FROM SURVIVING TO THRIVING

FROM SURVIVING TO THRIVING

NICK LAWRENCE

Contents

Dedication	viii
Preface	1
Introduction	4
Part I: Understanding Your Inner Landscape	11
1 The Language of Your Body	12
2 Your Internal Chemistry	26
3 The Dance of Your Brain	39
Part II: The Science of Feeling Safe	51
4 The Power of Perception	52
5 Your Nervous System Map	64
6 The Breath as Medicine	75
Part III: Practical Tools for Daily Life	87
7 Becoming Your Own Detective	88
8 Creating Your Happiness Hormone Calendar	98
9 The Art of Co-Regulation	110
Part IV: Breaking Generational Patterns	121
10 When the Past Lives in Your Body	122
11 Modeling Peace	131
12 Building Your Support Village	141
Conclusion: Your Legacy of Healing	155

Appendix A: Quick Reference Guides   165
Appendix B: Resources for Continued Learning   167
Chapter Summaries   169
Acknowledgements   172
In Gratitude   174

Copyright © 2025 by Nick Lawrence. MA
All rights reserved. No part of this book may be reproduced in any manner whatsoever without written permission except in the case of brief quotations embodied in critical articles and reviews.
First Printing, 2025

To Donna Lawrence, my wife:
You are the love of my life. Thank you for choosing to walk this journey of life with me, for believing in me and my gifts, and for helping me sit with my darkest childhood experiences. Thank you for helping me outline and edit this book; without you, there would be no book.

Preface

I am an educator. One of my biggest teacher gifts is the ability to take broad and diverse sets of complex information and break them down into bite-sized, easily digestible pieces for students. This book is the culmination of over thirty years of study in the complex fields of: human development, learning theories, neuroscience, biology, physiology, psychology, and metaphysics. In this book, these concepts are distilled into a gentle, easy-to-use system of how to think about yourself and others.

My goal is for you to see yourselves and your behaviors as indicators of how your nervous system is navigating your life. What happens to you everyday, the ways you engage with others, and how you think about life itself is your *navigational identity*. This identity is based on an amalgam of your deepest thoughts, feelings and beliefs, which get developed, usually, in early childhood. How we see the world, what we expect from family, how we view work or careers, what we deserve in terms of wealth, health, and joy, are all set into a deeply embedded, mechanized pattern that we become accustomed to and accept as *how life is*.

However, your navigational identity, and the mechanisms that keep it going, are not made in concrete, but in neuroplasticity; this means these mechanisms, and most importantly, your navigational identity can be changed. The work is simple, but not necessarily easy. You are the only one who can change your navigation system in yourself; you can teach others how to change it themselves. However, you cannot change it in or for another person. Nor can someone do this for you.

The study of the brain and the autonomic nervous system is at the foundation of this book. However, the book is not about either of those directly, but about how you are unconsciously utilizing the science that is inherent in both aspects. They are woven together in the most amazing ways. In fact, your whole body is a magnificent piece of complex art working on your behalf.

This book is about noticing. When you start to notice your internal sensations and begin to honor them, you will start being able to better guide your nervous system for the outcomes that you really want. So many people are going through the motions of life wondering, "Is this really all life has to offer?" And the answer, often, is "I hope not."

Life is just life; Life itself isn't personal. How we experience it *is* personal. It has ups and downs, good weather and bad weather, twisted ankles and the flu, glorious beach days and barbeques. Your experience of these events, life, depends completely on which part of your navigation system you are engaging with, despite what is actually happening. What I mean is you could have the flu but be happy that you get to stay home and binge watch something on TV. You could also have a terrible internal experience while at the beach when everyone else is really enjoying themselves.

Here is the key to living your life in the best way possible: Notice your internal physical sensations (your nervous system speaking to you), notice your external manifestations (quality of job, friends, family experiences), and ask yourself, "Is this really what I want? And if not, what exactly do I want?"

With these specific questions in mind, I have created a simple way to explain and recognize how to manage the science of both sides of your brain. For simplicity, I leave out the Amygdala and attribute some of its work to the right side of the brain. The Amygdala, housed in the brain stem, is a major processor of emotions and memories. However, I generalize the experience of emotions and memories to the right side of the brain, because the right side manages the fight-flight-freeze response.

I am particularly fond of metaphysics, the study of God in a personal yet scientific way. You will notice I make reference to God throughout the book. If you are uncomfortable with the word "God," feel free to change it to something more suitable for you. When I refer to God, I am referring to the creative force that gives us life, the ability to think, feel and imagine, and what I believe is the driving force in our consciousness, as living, sentient beings. I believe that God is present in all places and at all times. This means that God is right here in me, and right here in you as you read these words. This simple exercise is *Noticing the Presence of God*. If you can do this, you can do anything!

In terms of this book, I invite your questions, suggestions, and feedback, positive or negative. It took me over thirty years to put this all together and it isn't perfect. I look forward to hearing how my work helps you and how it doesn't help you. I want your feedback so I can make this book, and my subsequent work, as meaningful as possible. You see, in addition to being an educator, I am a lifelong learner. And you, my dear reader, are my student, which makes **you** my very best teacher.

In Gratitude,
Nick Lawrence

Introduction

Your Journey to Wholeness

If you're holding this book, chances are you've experienced more than your fair share of life's challenges. Maybe you're a caregiver feeling overwhelmed by the frequent demands of caring for others. Perhaps you're someone who has experienced trauma yourself, or you love someone who has. Maybe you're just tired of feeling like you're "walking on eggshells," never quite sure when the next emotional explosion will happen, either from someone else or from within yourself.

I want you to know something right from the start: you're not broken. Your responses make perfect sense. And healing is not only possible - it's your birthright.

My name is Nick, and I've spent decades studying how the human nervous system works. I did this because mine was really out of whack. I could see, clearly, that I had behaviors and reactions that were really different than most other people I knew. I knew there was something wrong and over the years, I realized I had some very deep beliefs about myself that were crippling my ability to live a happy life.

The most essential observation I made was this: The human nervous system is built with an internal, neutral coalition waiting for your direction. If your nervous system perceives and interprets danger, it becomes an army, armed and ready, for defense or attack. If your nervous system perceives and interprets safety, it becomes a cheering throng of moms and dads waving banners and cheering for you in your "Welcome Home" parade, with feelings of relaxation and glory. Your everyday perceptions and interpretations determine which coalition is activated at any moment; the way you can tell which one is active is based on your internal physical sensations.

The second but equally essential observation was that our physical sensations create a "feeling tone" of our overall experiences in life, determined by our most consistent experiences during our first few years of life. Unchecked, they have a tremendous life-long impact on us. These feeling tones speak to us through our internal physical sensations.

When someone asks me what my childhood was like, I get an immediate sinking feeling in the pit of my stomach. This is what I mean by feeling tone: a sense of dread. It doesn't mean I didn't also have good times; it means the summary of my experiences growing up is an uncomfortable feeling. These summaries, and we all have them, positive or negative, are directly related to our experience of, and our belief in, how life works, **now**, even though the summaries come from our **past**.

This is a crucial foundational tool for you to grab onto because how you felt then is likely how you are feeling now, even though your circumstances and conditions have changed. Your summary of how it feels for you to live your life is speaking to you through your daily physical sensations. So, if you don't like how you feel inside, sitting with and validating the particulars of how you actually do feel, even though uncomfortable, is the first step to rewiring your internal experience, which rewires your external expression of life. The inside is reflected in the outside; your inside experience is being mirrored back to you in your outside life, i.e. what you are manifesting as your day-to-day life.

The human nervous system is complex. I break it down into user-friendly ways by personifying it whenever possible. Let's start with the basics.

Think of a traffic light. When we are in our internal "Green Zone" called "Safety," our nervous system initiates the production of happiness hormones. When we move into our internal "Yellow Zone", called "Caution/Danger," Cortisol, our stress hormone gets initiated, and depending on the severity of the situation, gets ramped up, also releasing adrenaline, our super power. When we are in our internal "Red Zone" called "Danger/Life Threat," our nervous system realizes that we are in some form of impossible entrapment and then some kind of "Freeze" occurs, like depression, shutting down, disassociation, etc.

When this happens, depending on the severity of the life threat or perceived threat, your nervous system might make high levels of all of your hormones, making you suddenly calm and lucid, while still producing stress hormones. It's a form of self-preservation like playing dead. Numerous animals play dead just in this way: opossum, rabbits, certain snakes, certain fish, various insects and some birds like ducks. In these animals, automatic, involuntary responses can involve going limp, closing eyes, and even emitting foul odors to make the animal seem like a decaying, inedible meal.

However, while this is perfectly logical and obvious, knowing which zone you are in isn't always obvious from the inside. Which zone we are in most frequently has much less to do with what is happening now than what used to happen when we were young. I am talking specifically about registering a deep red zone response when such intensity of a response is not necessarily matching the actual circumstance. Which zones we live in and which hormones get produced, in general, our activated coalition, comes from our earliest circumstances, conditions and long-term training, from observing and experiencing the feeling tones and zones of our parents. Their way becomes our way as we are molded into deeply embedded patterns, THEIR PATTERNS, over time. In order to change your patterns, i.e. not turn out like your parents, you have to notice them, catch them and redirect them to your liking. This is what my book is about.

My journey into this work didn't start in a classroom or laboratory. It started in a violent household where I learned that the sound of bickering meant danger was coming. My nervous system developed an exquisite sensitivity to tension because it needed to in order to keep me safe. If I were to draw a picture of the traffic light that dominated my early years, it would have a tiny green zone, an enormous yellow zone and a big red zone. Perhaps you have or had a similar experience. Drawing your own traffic light representing your childhood experiences is an excellent way to prepare yourself for the exercises in this book.

As a child, when at my friend's house, his parents would sometimes bicker; he'd roll his eyes and turn up the TV. But me? I'd feel that familiar tightness in my chest, my heart racing, the need to flee. Similar parental bickering, two different perceptions, and outcomes, but my nervous system didn't know that. Perception is one of the most important concepts we'll explore together. Why? Because it happens faster than thinking and it initiates our hormonal responses that determine which zone we are in and which coalition gets activated.

This book isn't about erasing your past or pretending trauma doesn't have lasting effects. It's about understanding that your nervous system learned to protect you in whatever way it could, and those protective patterns made perfect sense then. Now, with gentle awareness and some practical tools, you can honor what kept you safe while creating new patterns that serve you better.

What You'll Discover

In these pages, you'll learn about the sophisticated communication system happening inside your body every moment of every day. You'll discover that when you feel that familiar "yucky feeling" - whether it's tightness in your jaw, heaviness in your chest, or that stomach-dropping sensation - it's not a character flaw. It's your nervous system flooding your body with stress hormones because it perceives danger.

You'll also learn about the magical cocktail of happiness hormones your body can produce when it feels safe: Dopamine (your satisfaction hormone), Endorphins (your natural pain relief), Oxytocin (your connection hormone), and Serotonin (your feel-good hormone). These aren't just nice concepts; they're actual chemicals that can, and do, transform how you experience daily life. The goal is to notice when you have, or are having, a caution or danger response that isn't actually appropriate at the moment, how to turn it off, and turn on your happiness hormones instead. This is you managing the science of your body for you, instead of being a victim of a hypersensitive danger response that got developed in you, but not consciously made by you. This is where your free will comes into play.

Most importantly, you'll learn practical tools you can use right now: The 4-10 breathing technique that can literally switch off stress hormone production; the activity analysis method that helps you identify what's draining your energy unnecessarily, and the co-regulation principles that can help your entire family feel safer.

A Note About the Process

Healing trauma isn't like fixing a broken appliance where you follow a manual and everything works perfectly afterward. It's more like tending a garden - it requires patience, consistency, and gentleness with yourself. Have you ever noticed a blossom on a plant when you know it wasn't there the day before? That's how all living things grow: in bursts, and you and your loved ones will grow in bursts, too.

Some days you'll remember to breathe deeply, remembering to focus on your elongated exhales, gently reminding your nervous system to go back to making happiness hormones. Others you'll wonder angrily how you ever agreed to marry the most irritating person in the world! Ha ha! That's just life! The most likely explanation is that you and your spouse are both perceiving danger at the same time and you accidentally blame each other for your own internal experiences. As you develop these skills, you will be able to feel that first sign of stress, and you'll marvel at how quickly you return to calm. Other days you'll find yourself in a full stress response before you even realize what happened. Both are normal. Both are part of the process.

I've worked with foster parents who were so burned out they could barely function, former foster youth trying to break cycles of trauma, and families dealing with everything from anxiety disorders to the aftermath of violence. What I've learned is that small, consistent changes in how we relate to our nervous system can create profound shifts not just in our own lives, but in the lives of everyone around us. And that is co-regulation at its finest!

Your Nervous System's Wisdom

Throughout this book, I want you to remember that your nervous system isn't your enemy. It's been working tirelessly to keep you alive and as safe as possible given the circumstances you've faced. When it floods you with cortisol (stress hormone) at what seems like the "wrong" time, it's because some part of your experience has triggered an alarm that says "danger."

The goal isn't to never feel stress or never get triggered. That isn't possible; just like you can't take the instinct out of a wolf. The goal is to develop what I call "nervous system awareness" - the ability to notice when you're moving out of your green zone (safety) and into your yellow zone (caution/danger) or red zone (danger/life threat), and to have tools to gently guide yourself back to safety.

How to Use This Book

This book is designed to be both educational and immediately practical. Each chapter builds on the previous one, but you can also jump to specific sections based on what you need most right now. If you're in crisis, you might want to start with Chapter 6 on breathing techniques. If you're curious about the science behind everything, Part I will give you that foundation.

Throughout the book, you'll find stories from my work with clients (names and details changed to protect privacy), examples from my own life, and practical exercises you can try. Please be gentle with yourself as you read. If something brings up difficult emotions, that's your nervous system giving you information. You can always put the book down, take some clearing breaths, and come back when you're ready.

A Personal Promise

I promise you this: the tools in this book work. Not because I'm some guru with all the answers, but because they're based on how your nervous system actually functions. When you understand that your difficult emotions are physiology, not personality flaws, everything *changes for you*. When you understand that your child's intense, emotional outburst is their physiology, not personality flaws, everything changes in *how you see them*. When your child understands that their own intense, emotional outbursts are their physiology and not something wrong about them, everything *changes for them and how they see themselves!* This single bit of knowledge has radically affected how struggling students saw themselves as learners in college. They thought they weren't good at learning when in fact, their nervous systems were just on high alert and they couldn't take anything else in.

How many of us have been beaten down externally while taking a beating internally? Seeing behaviors as nervous system communication is key to feeling better. When you learn to work with your nervous system instead of against it, you stop exhausting yourself fighting battles you were never meant to fight alone. And you stop condemning your kids for something they likely simply cannot control.

Your healing matters. Not just to you, but to everyone whose life you touch. When you learn to return to your own green zone, you become what I call a "regulator" for others - someone who helps everyone else feel safer just by being present. This is how we break generational patterns of trauma. This is how we create families and communities where everyone can thrive.

Are you ready to begin? Exhale with a whoosh sound. Flare your nostrils and breath into fullness followed by a slow exhale to complete emptiness. Do this a few times, focusing on elongating your exhales. You are going to learn to make your breath your ally in the most important work you'll ever do: coming home to yourself, and helping others to come home to themselves. This is the purpose of my life's work. By the way, when we are at home within ourselves, deep in our "green zone," we are able to hear the voice of God speaking to us, guiding us. What could be more important than that?

Part I: Understanding Your Inner Landscape

"The body keeps the score."
— *Bessel van der Kolk*

1

The Language of Your Body

Recognizing Safety and Danger Signals

Your body is constantly talking to you. Every moment of every day, it's sending signals through physical sensations, letting you know whether you're safe or in danger. We are designed to feel good, so most people don't really notice feeling good. The problem is, most of us were never taught to listen to this language, particularly the danger messages. Why? Because low level danger comes through as frustration, worry or concern. Which, when translated to child-speak can sound and feel a lot like clinging and whining, which parents misinterpret as manipulative.

When I was a child, we used to visit my great-grandmother at her retirement home. Every time she saw me she greeted me with great warmth, but she would kiss me right on my ear on both sides, making loud smootchy noises and it would cause me great pain. It happened once after I had an ear infection and I screamed and ran and hid.

Even though she would always give me a chocolate bar, I developed pre-danger anxiety as soon as we were in the car on our way to see her. I told my mother, but instead of asking grandma to kiss me somewhere else, like on my cheek or top of my head, my mother thought I was just being difficult and told me Grandma didn't mean to hurt me.

This is one of the ways I learned that my comfort wasn't important. I KNEW that she didn't mean to hurt me, but I needed help in making sure *she didn't continue* to hurt me. I needed my mom to say, "Of course I will make sure she understands. I want you to enjoy seeing her."

So many of us were taught to push through, to ignore what our bodies were telling us, to override our own internal wisdom to not hurt someone else's feelings or "make a scene." This is an exceptionally important concept for you to understand. The ramifications of ignoring our own internal wisdom accumulate and multiply, like a giant snowball, over the course of our lives. Then, unnoticed, we do the exact same thing to our own children, perpetuating harm for no reason at all.

But what if I told you that those sensations - the tightness in your jaw when you're frustrated, the heaviness in your chest when you're worried, the sinking feeling in your stomach when you're scared - are actually sophisticated communications from your nervous system? What if learning to understand this language could change everything about how you experience life?

Let me tell you about Rebecca, one of my foster parent students. She came to my class completely exhausted, describing herself as "an army of one" trying to manage everything in her life. When I asked the class to notice their physical sensations for feeling safe versus feeling stressed, Rebecca had a profound realization.

"For feeling safe," she said, "I honestly can't remember the last time I felt that way." When she tried to connect with what safety might feel like in her body, she could barely find it. But for stress? "Tight everywhere. Heavy. Like I'm carrying the world on my shoulders."

This was a light bulb moment for Rebecca. She suddenly understood that she had been living in a state of chronic stress for so long that it felt normal. Her body had been trying to tell her "Hey, we need rest, we need support, we need to feel safe," but she had learned to interpret those signals as weakness or laziness rather than as important information.

The Quick Write Exercise

Before we go any deeper, I want you to do the same exercise I do with all my students. Get a piece of paper and something to write with. I'm going to give you some feelings to focus upon. Your job is to notice what physical sensations, words, or images come up in your body and write them down. I really recommend getting a journal specifically for reading this book. That way you can watch yourself grow as you attend to this part of your experience. Go to a quiet space, outside and inside, so you can really pay attention to what comes up. Whatever comes up during this exercise is of great importance to your healing journey. The first half is a green zone exercise. If you only have yellow/red zone feelings come up, just write them down and follow the activity. Then skip to chapter 10 for further instructions.

Part 1: The three feelings we are focusing on are: safety, confidence, and freedom. I want you to say to yourself, "I am safe." Notice what happens and write it down. Then say, "I am confident." Again, notice what physical sensations, words or images come up in your body, and write it down. Then say, "I am free," and write down what you notice. If you have a hard time noticing or remembering what these states of being feel like, or if you only have negative things come up, ask yourself to safe, confident and free just notice them, thank them and write them down.

Don't think about this too intently - feel it or imagine it. We're looking for physical sensations like:

- Relaxation in your muscles

- Deeper breathing
- Calmness
- Lower heart rate
- A sense of lightness or expansion
- Warmth spreading through your body
- A settling or grounding feeling

Part 2: Now think about feeling frustrated, afraid, or trapped. Say "I feel frustrated." Notice what physical sensations and words or images come up in your body, and write them down. Then say, "I feel afraid." Notice what happens, and write it down. And finally say, "I feel trapped." Write down your internal experience. Many people who have experienced trauma find it much easier to describe their internal sensations relating to feeling frustrated, afraid or trapped than feelings of safety, confidence and freedom.

You might notice:

- Tightness anywhere in your body
- Constriction or heaviness
- Changes in your breathing (holding your breath, shallow breathing)
- A sense of shrinking or contracting
- Tension in your jaw, shoulders, or stomach
- Increased heart rate
- Sinking feeling in your chest or stomach

Take your time with this. These sensations are your personal dashboard, and they're about to become one of your most important tools for healing.

Understanding Your Personal Dashboard

Just like your car has a dashboard that tells you important information - when you're low on gas, when your engine is overheating, when your blinker is on - your body has a dashboard, too. Those physical sensations are like warning lights letting you know what's happening with your nervous system.

When Kerry, another student, did this exercise, she discovered something fascinating. "When I feel safe," she said, "I notice slow, easy breathing. Like everything just... settles." But when she thought about feeling frustrated, "I clench my jaw every time."

This was huge information for Kerry. By recognizing her physical sensation as a dashboard indicator, she became aware of her own early warning system. The moment she noticed her jaw clenching, she could think, "Oh, my nervous system is picking up on something that feels like danger. Let me pay attention to what's happening and see if I need to take care of myself." This awareness allowed her to not take out her increasing tightness on her family.

Rachel had a similar breakthrough. "I hold my breath when I'm anxious," she realized. "I probably spend half my day holding my breath and don't even know it." This awareness alone began to change things for her. She started noticing when she was holding her breath and would consciously choose to exhale slowly, which naturally calmed her nervous system.

The Science Behind the Sensations

Here's what's happening when you notice these physical changes: your nervous system is constantly scanning your internal and external environment for signs of safety or danger. This scanning happens below the level of conscious thought - it's happening right now as you read this.

When your nervous system perceives safety, it activates what's called your parasympathetic nervous system - your "rest and digest" mode, also known as your "Green Zone." When the parasympathetic nervous system is dominating your experience through the lens of safety, your body produces happiness hormones and you feel those pleasant sensations like relaxation, warmth, and ease. This is directly related to your Vagus Nerve and is managed by the left side of your brain. It is also how you are able to hear the voice of God, from within your rest and digest mode.

When your nervous system perceives danger (and remember, it doesn't have to be actual danger - just the perception of danger), it activates your sympathetic nervous system - your "fight, flight, or freeze" mode. This floods your body with stress hormones like cortisol, which creates those uncomfortable sensations like tightness, heaviness, and constriction. These self-defense mechanisms are managed by the sympathetic nervous system that is managed by the right side of your brain.

God, in God's amazing wisdom, gave us a way to ensure our own longevity. This is why our fight-flight-freeze mode takes over and is louder than anything else when in danger. The brilliant thing about your nervous system is that it's always trying to keep you safe. The challenging thing is that it makes these determinations based on past experiences, which means it might perceive danger when you're actually safe now.

Too many people get stuck there, in danger mode, due to those deep patterns that get developed over time. I used to be one of them and that is why I am inviting you to practice the skills that get you back home to God within you.

Why This Matters for Trauma

If you've experienced trauma, your nervous system likely learned that the world isn't always safe. It developed what we might call "hypervigilance" - an increased sensitivity to potential threats. This was adaptive; it helped keep you safe in situations that truly were dangerous.

But here's where it gets tricky: your nervous system doesn't automatically update its threat assessment when your circumstances change. Just like our electronic devices, we have to consciously update them. The same is true for your nervous system. If you learned early in life that raised voices mean violence is coming, your nervous system might still flood you with stress hormones every time someone raises their voice - even if it's just excitement or enthusiasm.

Amanda, one of my students, had a powerful insight about this. She realized that most of her stress responses were happening around activities with her kids. "I was surprised to see how much stuff around the kids was heavily in the red," she shared. This wasn't because she didn't love her children, but because her nervous system had learned to be hyperalert around the needs and emotions of others.

Creating Your Personal Checklist

Now that you have a better understanding of your personal dashboard, I want you to turn your observations into a practical tool. Take what you wrote down about your physical sensations and turn them into questions like the ones listed below so you can check in with yourself throughout the day:

Green Zone Checklist (Safety):

- Am I feeling calm in my body?
- Is my breathing slow and easy?
- Do I feel relaxed in my muscles?
- Is there a sense of lightness or ease?

Yellow/Red Zone Checklist (Stress):

- Am I feeling tight anywhere?
- Is my jaw clenched?
- Am I holding my breath?
- Do I feel heavy or constricted?

The goal isn't to never experience stress sensations - that's not realistic or even healthy. The goal is awareness. When you notice you're in your yellow or red zone, you can think, "Oh, my nervous system is activated right now. Let me see what's going on and how I can take care of myself."

The Power of Simply Noticing

One of the most common questions I get is, "But what do I do when I notice I'm stressed?" And sometimes the answer is surprisingly simple: just notice. Without judgment, without trying to fix it, just acknowledge what's happening.

You might say to yourself, "I notice I'm feeling really tight in my shoulders right now. My nervous system is activated." That's it. You're not trying to make it go away or figure out why it's happening. You're just developing the skill of awareness. Awareness is a form of validation. Validation is often the key to being able to breathe out fully, the most direct path to relaxation.

However, validating your experience might not be enough. The most important action to take after noticing, is to EXHALE completely, then breathe into fullness, before exhaling slowly again. I flare my nostrils when breathing in and then breathe out slowly, through my mouth, like I'm blowing through a straw. Flaring my nostrils reminds me to keep breathing.

Now whenever I get upset, just the act of flaring my nostrils brings me the ability to breathe and relax better. Depending on how upset you are, you may not be able to breathe in for long at first. However, by focusing on your elongated exhale, you are telling the right side of your brain, the fight-flight-or freeze side, that everything is ok and to enter the state of rest and digest. It is simply the most direct route to your own green zone.

These two steps (noticing and breathing) might seem too simple to matter, but I promise you their effect is profound. Many of us spend so much energy fighting our own sensations or judging ourselves for having them. When you can simply notice, acknowledge and breathe into what's happening, you stop wasting energy on that internal battle and can start responding from a place of self-compassion and compassion for others.

Working with Your Loved Ones

Once you understand your own dashboard, you can start helping your loved ones understand theirs. This is especially important if you're caring for children who have experienced trauma. Their nervous systems might be even more sensitive to perceived threats than yours is.

One of my clients, a foster parent, learned to ask his kids, "What does your body feel like right now?" instead of "Why are you acting this way?" or "Stop doing that right now or I will take your skateboard away." This simple shift acknowledged that their behaviors were connected to what they were experiencing internally, not (assumed) choices they were making to be difficult.

You can teach children to notice things like:

- "My tummy feels tight"
- "My heart is beating fast"
- "I feel shaky"
- "My body feels heavy"

When children learn that these sensations are information rather than something to be ashamed of, they can start to work with their nervous system instead of against it. Everyone in your family will start to really appreciate honesty in a new way and you will see a new kind of closeness emerge as you and your people start to relax together.

Common Misconceptions

Let me address a few things I hear often in my classes:

"I should be able to control my stress responses." Actually, no. These responses happen faster than conscious thought. You can't control them, but you can learn to work with them.

"If I'm safe now, I shouldn't feel afraid." Your nervous system doesn't operate on logic. It operates on pattern recognition. If something reminds it of a past danger, it will respond as if that danger is present now.

"Strong people don't get triggered." This is completely backwards. Sensitive nervous systems often belong to people who have survived incredible challenges. That sensitivity was part of what kept you alive.

Building Your Awareness Practice

Start small. For the next week, I want you to check in with your body three times a day. Maybe when you first wake up, sometime in the afternoon, and before bed. Just ask yourself:

- What do I notice in my body right now?
- Does this feel more like safety or stress?
- What might my nervous system be responding to?

Don't try to change anything yet. Just practice the skill of noticing. This is like building a muscle - it gets stronger with practice.

Remember, your body's signals are not your enemy. They're information. They're your nervous system's way of trying to take care of you. When you learn to listen to this language with curiosity rather than judgment, you're taking the first crucial step toward healing.

Mapping Your Personal Traffic Light

I want you to become a detective of your own nervous system. Think about yesterday or maybe the day before - pick a day when you felt like you were riding an emotional roller coaster.

When Your System Hits Yellow or Red: Close your eyes for a moment and remember how your body felt during the most stressful part of that day. Did your jaw clench like you were holding back words you wanted to scream? Did your chest feel like someone was sitting on it? Maybe your breathing got so shallow you forgot you even needed air? Or perhaps you felt that familiar sensation of being "revved up" like a car engine that won't turn off?

Write these sensations down. Your body has been trying to tell you something important, and it's sending you an invitation to start listening.

When You Found Your Green Zone: Now shift your attention to a moment when you felt genuinely at peace. Maybe it was when you laughed so hard your belly hurt, or during those precious minutes when you stepped outside and just breathed. Perhaps it was after you finished something that mattered to you and felt that sweet satisfaction.

What did safety feel like in your body? Did your shoulders drop like they were finally allowed to rest? Could you suddenly breathe all the way down to your toes? Did you feel lighter, like someone had lifted an invisible weight off your chest?

Your Personal Alarm Triggers: Here's where it gets really interesting. What sends your nervous system into high alert? Is it when someone uses that particular tone of voice that makes your skin crawl? When plans change at the last minute and you feel like the rug's been pulled out from under you? Maybe it's certain environments that make you want to run for the hills?

There's absolutely no shame in having triggers - we all have them. You're just getting curious about what yours are.

Going Deeper: Questions for Your Heart

Your Childhood Body Memory: I want you to try something. Think about your childhood and notice what happens in your body before your mind starts analyzing. Do you get that warm, expansive feeling like a hug from the inside? Or do you feel that familiar sinking sensation in your stomach, like mine? Maybe it's something else entirely - tightness, heaviness, or even numbness.

Whatever you notice is perfect information about how your nervous system learned to navigate the world.

Becoming Your Own Zone Tracker: For the next three days, I want you to check in with yourself like you're taking your emotional temperature. Not to fix anything or judge what you find, but just to notice. "Hmm, what zone am I hanging out in right now? What might have nudged me here?"

Think of yourself as a loving scientist studying the most fascinating subject in the world - you.

The Nervous Systems That Raised You: This one might bring up some feelings, and that's okay. Think about the adults who were around you most when you were little. Were they usually in their green zone - calm, present, able to handle whatever came their way? Or did they live more in yellow and red - stressed, reactive, always bracing for the next crisis?

Remember, they were doing their absolute best with their own nervous system programming. You absorbed their patterns not because anyone did anything wrong, but because that's how little humans learn - by watching and feeling what the big humans around them do.

Your Safety Anchors: This is my favorite question because it's about what already works for you. What are the people, places, activities, or experiences that reliably help your nervous system remember that you're safe?

Maybe it's your dog's unconditional love, or that one friend who never makes you feel like you have to perform. Perhaps it's being in nature, or the ritual of your morning coffee, or that song that always makes you feel like everything's going to be okay.

These are your green zone anchors - treat them like the precious resources they are. Your nervous system needs these touchstones to remember what safety feels like.

Take your time with these questions. There's no rush, no right answers, and definitely no judgment. You're simply getting acquainted with the brilliant, complex system that's been working so hard to keep you safe all these years.

Exercise: Your Personal Zone Map

Take a moment to reflect on your own internal traffic light. Think about a recent day when you felt particularly stressed or overwhelmed.

Yellow/Red Zone Moments: What physical sensations did you notice? Was it the familiar tightness in your jaw? Heaviness in your chest? Shallow breathing? The feeling of being "wound up" or "on edge"? Write down what your body does when it's not feeling safe.

Green Zone Moments: Now think about a time when you felt genuinely calm and at peace. Maybe it was after a good laugh with a friend, during a quiet moment in nature, or after completing something meaningful. What did that feel like in your body? Relaxed shoulders? Deeper breathing? A sense of lightness or expansion?

Your Triggers: What situations, sounds, or interactions tend to move you from green into yellow or red? Common triggers include certain tones of voice, feeling rushed, unexpected changes in plans, or specific environments. There's no judgment here - just noticing patterns.

Journal Prompts for Deeper Reflection

1. **Childhood Feeling Tone:** When you think about your childhood, what immediate sensation do you notice in your body? Does it feel warm and expansive, heavy and constrictive, or something else entirely? This is valuable information about your nervous system's baseline programming.

2. **Daily Zone Patterns:** Track your zones for three days. Simply notice: What zone am I in right now? What might have influenced this shift? You're not trying to change anything yet - just developing awareness.

3. **Family Zone Legacy:** Think about the adults who raised you. Which zones did they seem to live in most often? How did they handle stress or conflict? Remember, they were doing their best with their own nervous system programming, and you absorbed those patterns through observation.

4. **Safety Anchors:** What people, places, activities, or experiences reliably help you feel safer and more grounded? These are your green zone anchors - precious resources for nervous system regulation.

Take your time with these questions. There's no rush, no right answers, and definitely no judgment. You're simply getting acquainted with the brilliant, complex system that's been working so hard to keep you safe all these years.

2

Your Internal Chemistry

How Happiness and Stress Hormones Shape Your World

Imagine your body has two different medicine cabinets. One contains the most beautiful, healing medicines you could ever want - natural mood elevators, pain relievers, connection enhancers, and joy producers. The other contains emergency medications designed for crisis situations - stimulants that can give you superhuman strength, focus enhancers for life-or-death situations, and alarm systems that mobilize every resource you have.

Both medicine cabinets serve important purposes. The first - what I call your happiness hormone cabinet - is designed for daily life, for thriving, for connecting with others and enjoying your experience of being alive. The second - your stress hormone cabinet - is designed for emergencies, for survival, for getting you through genuine crises.

The challenge many of us face is that our nervous system has gotten confused about when and which medicine cabinet to use. We find ourselves reaching for the emergency medications during everyday situations, burning through our body's resources at an unsustainable rate.

Meet Your Happiness Hormones

Let me introduce you to your natural pharmacy of wellness. These aren't just nice concepts - they're actual chemicals your body produces that can transform how you experience life.

Dopamine is your satisfaction hormone. It's what floods your system when you set a goal and achieve it, when you accomplish something meaningful, when you experience that "Yes! I did it!" feeling. Dopamine is what motivates you to keep going, to try new things, to pursue what matters to you. When dopamine is low, people feel like they are in a stressed mess and feel overwhelmed by everyday life.

Endorphins are your body's natural morphine. The word literally means "internal morphine"--*endo* (inside) and *orphine* (from morphine). These are your mood and pain regulators. When you laugh until your stomach hurts, when you exercise intensely, when you feel that natural high from moving your body or work with others to achieve something challenging, that's endorphins. When endorphins are low, people feel lethargic and weak and have low energy.

Oxytocin is what I call, "The Great Soother." When you release oxytocin, the most soothing feeling flows through your brain and into your body. It's like having the most loving, accepting parent you could imagine saying, "Oh, I love you so much. You're going to be okay." Oxytocin is the foundation of co-regulation and gets released when nursing a baby, cradling a baby, holding a loved one, saying, "awwww" or "ohhhhh" when the other person is upset. While you are *helping* them feel better, you aren't actually *making* them feel better. What you are doing is educating their nervous system on how to self-soothe by helping them *release oxytocin in themselves.*

Releasing oxytocin is one of the most important ways you teach someone to recover from emotional pain and be able to manage their emotions. People who receive this training are able to soothe themselves the fastest, not get hung up on failures or setbacks, and have the most tenacity and grit. When low in oxytocin, people feel alone even when surrounded by caring loved ones. People that are able to self-soothe feel cared for and loved even when in complete isolation.

Serotonin is your feel-good hormone. When you have optimal serotonin, life feels good. You wake up thinking, "What a beautiful day!" You see the world through a lens of possibility and gratitude. When serotonin is low, it's like being under a dark cloud where nothing looks bright or hopeful.

Your Stress Response System

Meet Your Primary Stress Hormone

Now let's talk about your stress hormone system, which centers around **cortisol**. Cortisol isn't bad - it's essential for life. It's what gets you out of bed in the morning, what gets you to the airport on time; it helps you respond to genuine emergencies, and mobilizes your internal resources when you truly need them.

But cortisol is designed for short bursts, not constant activation. Think of it like the turbo boost in a car - incredible when you need it, but if you tried to drive that way all the time, you'd burn out your engine. Caregivers are notorious for developing health issues usually seen in much older people because they are burning through their internal resources at a much faster rate than intended by our human design, i.e. driving in overdrive too often.

When cortisol floods your system, it creates those physical sensations we talked about in Chapter 1 - the tightness, the heaviness, the constriction. But here's what's really important to understand: that horrible feeling you get before you cry, that awful sensation that hurts so bad you sob - that's massive amounts of cortisol. It's not weakness or manipulation. It's physiology.

The Real-Life Impact

Let me tell you about one of my students who took the hormone assessment I use in my classes. Her scores were sobering - high across the board for deficiencies in happiness hormones. When she shared her results with the group, she said, "My scores were all terrible. Oh, I mean like... I definitely knew I was struggling, but I didn't realize how badly I was struggling. At first I felt ashamed that my scores were so high, but now I am grateful to have this insight. I really didn't know I could do anything about how I was feeling. I was told for so many years that there was something wrong with me. Learning how to recognize my physical internal sensations as simple messages and not faults saved my life."

This brave honesty opened up a conversation for the whole class about how many of us are walking around severely depleted in our natural wellness chemistry, often without realizing it. We've adapted to running on stress hormones for so long that it feels normal. And it is exhausting.

Rebecca, the student I mentioned earlier who described herself as "an army of one," had a similar awakening. Her high scores weren't a character judgment - they were just feedback; information about what her nervous system had been experiencing. When you're frequently in survival mode, trying to manage everything alone, your body stops producing the chemicals that help you thrive and starts producing the chemicals that help you survive. And this is no way to live!

Why This Happens

Your nervous system produces either happiness hormones or stress hormones based on your perception of safety or danger in any given moment. Notice I said perception, not reality. You don't have to actually be in danger to produce stress hormones - just the slightest perception that you might be is enough.

This is where trauma history becomes so relevant. If your early experiences taught your nervous system that the world is generally unsafe, it might default to stress hormone production even in situations that are objectively safe.

As you know, I grew up in a violent household, and my nervous system learned that bickering between adults was a sign that violence was predictably on its way. Even now, decades later, if I hear people start to argue, my body floods with cortisol. But now I know how to recognize it and within a minute or two, I am calm and relaxed because I am honoring the signals. I literally talk to the right side of my brain to help it calm down.

I have a cousin who died of an overdose. His name was Freddy. I named my right brain, while in fight-flight-or freeze, Freddy, after him. Maybe this sounds morbid, but to me it makes perfect sense. My family was fraught with mangled, explosive experiences. The real Freddy reminds me that I have to pay careful attention to my internal physical responses and to the warning signals the right side of my brain sends me.

When I get upset, I say, "Hey, Freddy, I've got you!" Then I breathe out to complete emptiness, flare my nostrils, and breathe into fullness. I do this for as long as it takes until I feel myself come into my green zone. I've got it down to a science now, and with practice, you will, too!

The Happiness Hormone Calendar

One of the most practical tools I've developed is what I call the Happiness Hormone Calendar. Instead of trying to add more to your already full life, this approach helps you be intentional about activities you're probably already doing, but with awareness of how they affect your internal chemistry. Below is an introduction to each hormone. I discuss this further in chapter eight.

Monday - Dopamine Day: Focus on setting and achieving goals. This could be as simple as making a list of what you want to accomplish and checking things off. The key is making your goals small enough that you can actually achieve them and get that dopamine hit.

Instead of "clean the whole house," try "clean the kitchen" so you get the satisfaction of completion. Then, and here is the most important part: Celebrate! Say, "**Who** did it? *I* did it!" over and over until you start to giggle. Dopamine is a teeter-totter with Serotonin (Friday); once dopamine is released, serotonin immediately says, "Of course you did!"

Tuesday - Endorphin Day: Incorporate movement, laughter, and sensory pleasure. This might be a yoga class, dancing to music you love, watching something funny, or even eating a piece of dark chocolate mindfully. Endorphins love intensity and group activities, like badass athletics, team sports and hard work, like digging, pulling and pushing.

Why? Because these activities simulate the fight-flight-freeze response in a safe environment, where you get to practice being in those situations where there are rules and time limits. Endorphins get stored like a savings account and you can draw from them when in actual danger situations.

If you do not have endorphins in your internal savings account, you get overdrawn and Adrenaline gets utilized. Adrenaline is the high powered gas engine that burns through fuel. Endorphins are like electricity, high-powered with plenty of power to get the job done. Cortisol and Adrenaline are like gasoline and burn much hotter.

Wednesday - Cortisol Day: Participate in activities that please your senses and encourage you to slow down like cooking, resting, making art, laughing, spending quality time (mutually agreed upon activities) with someone, enjoying nature and listening to music. This is the day to consciously seek your green zone. Focus on your elongated exhales and smiling to yourself and others. Say to yourself, "Things are going well. I am excited and grateful for all that I have."

Thursday- Oxytocin Day: Focus on connection and safe touch. This could be holding hands, giving or receiving hugs, caring for pets, or even just texting someone you care about to let them know you're thinking of them. It's also a great day to celebrate your or your loved ones' achievements by saying, "Ahhhhh" or "Wowwww" with a pitch from high to low. This sound activates the release of oxytocin in everyone.

Friday - Serotonin Day: Prioritize positive thinking, mindfulness, and time in nature. This might be a walking meditation, sitting in your garden, practicing gratitude, or simply noticing three things you appreciate about your day. This is a great day to offer affirmations to your loved ones and to receive them. Say things like, "Honey, I am so glad you were born!" or "Honey, I appreciate you so much!"

The beauty of this approach is that you're not adding new time consuming things to your week - you're bringing intention to things you probably already incorporate into your existing life.

Understanding Your Personal Deficits

In my classes, I have people take an assessment that helps them identify which happiness hormones they're most deficient in. The questions are based on symptoms that thousands of people have reported when they're low in four specific happiness hormones and high in cortisol, the main stress hormone.

For example, if you often feel depressed, bored, or like you've lost interest in things you used to enjoy, you might be low in dopamine. If you're dealing with frequent exhaustion, chronic pain, have difficulty recovering from exercise, or a loss of joy, endorphins might be your focus area.

One of my clients discovered through this assessment that his highest deficiency was in dopamine. He had been setting huge, overwhelming goals for himself and then feeling like a failure when he couldn't achieve them. When he learned to break his big goals into smaller, achievable pieces, he started getting regular dopamine hits that motivated him to keep going. In fact, an internal hit of dopamine also has a positive effect on serotonin, the "feel good" hormone. They feed off of each other, so a little intentional planning followed by a little intentional celebration starts a cascade of happiness hormone production inside of you. When you have this going on, you can literally tackle almost anything!

Another client found out she was severely low in oxytocin - the connection hormone. She was surrounded by people who loved her but still felt profoundly lonely. Understanding this helped her recognize that she needed safe, wanted physical touch and quality time with others to feel truly connected. Connection is the foundation of health in this order: Connection to God, connection to Self, connection to others. This is accomplished most directly through the conscientious decrease in cortisol and increase in oxytocin..

The Cortisol Connection

Now, here's where it gets interesting. Sometimes people have high cortisol scores but normal happiness hormone scores. This might mean they're stressed about something specific, but their overall well-being chemistry is okay. Other times, people are low in happiness hormones but have normal cortisol. This could indicate depression or burnout without a specific stressor.

But when both are off - when you have deficient happiness hormones and elevated stress hormones - that's when life feels really, really hard. Everything is a struggle, few things bring you joy, and you're frequently operating from a place of depletion.

This is especially common in caregivers, people who have experienced trauma, and anyone who has been in chronic stress for extended periods. The good news is that once you understand what's happening, you can start to address it systematically.

Working with Your Chemistry, Not Against It

One of the biggest misconceptions I encounter is that we should be able to think our way out of hormonal imbalances. "I know I have a good life, so why do I feel so bad?" people ask. But feelings aren't logic problems - they're chemistry.

If you're low in serotonin, positive thinking becomes incredibly difficult because you literally don't have the brain chemistry to support optimistic thoughts. If you're high in cortisol, your creativity and problem-solving abilities are compromised because your brain is in survival mode. This experience leaves people feeling alone and scared. When you have low cortisol, you feel lighter, easier-going, and able to connect.

This is why I always start with the basics: breathing techniques that focus on the elongated exhale to regulate the nervous system, simple activities to support happiness hormone production, and lifestyle changes that reduce unnecessary cortisol activation.

The Ripple Effect

Here's something beautiful about working with your internal chemistry: it doesn't just affect you. When you're producing happiness hormones, you become what I call an "emotional regulator" for others. Your calm, grounded presence helps other people's nervous systems settle. Think of yourself like a radio, emitting a particular frequency.

This frequency might sound like Country Western music or Classical music, etc. In terms of your family, your frequency might sound like a twanging reminder or a lovely melody. Sometimes it sounds like Heavy Metal or Grunge music depending on what is happening.

If everyone is on the Classical music frequency and one person dives into loud angry Heavy Metal, one of two things will happen: either the whole group will also plunge into angry Heavy Metal, (and the "heavy metaler" becomes the regulator or driver) or the the Classical music will just gently keep on going and the heavy metaler will co-regulate and join in the Classical music frequency.

It is your job to be the conscientious emotional regulator in your family. It doesn't mean you have to be perfect all the time. It means that as soon as you notice that your family's frequency is going in an uncomfortable direction, apply your breathing technique to yourself and regulate yourself to the frequency you want. The more you practice this, the better you will be at it, and your family will also gladly join you.

This is especially important if you're parenting or caring for others who have experienced trauma. Children and trauma survivors are often hypervigilant to the emotional states of the adults around them. When you're flooded with stress hormones, they pick up on that and their nervous systems activate in response.

This means *your* reaction to *their* behaviors becomes the driving force, that you become the emotional regulator based on getting thrown off by your child's reaction. They come to you for support but it sounds like they are attacking you. You get angry and accidentally take the bait.

For example, you ask, "Honey, have you done your homework?" and your child barks back, angrily, "Why are you always on my back? Leave me alone!"

A common parental response is, "How dare you speak to me in that tone! You are NOT going to the basketball game!"

Now *you* are angry and have co-regulated to *their* initial uncomfortable frequency. It's you, not them. This is a skill that is difficult to catch at first because it really seems like they are causing all of the upset. When, in fact, they came to you dysregulated and you dove in.

Let's be clear: you will dive in. We all do. The truth is, in those moments, you have to keep your own "Ouch" to yourself and pause for a moment acknowledging they are having a big reaction to a common and supportive question.

"Are you stressing about your homework?" is a better response. But, even if you start with, "How dare you...", as soon as you notice yourself doing that you can say "PAUSE!" and then ask if they are stressed about their homework. They will be glad and might even offer an apology for barking at you earlier when given the time and space to cool off. Even though it may feel uncomfortable initially for some, we all need time and space to cool off; it is simply how a right brain flood recedes. Picking at someone who is having a right brain flood is the best way to exacerbate the issue. Notice what you do to others while they are attempting to calm themselves down. It is quite helpful to have an "I love you" message written down in the place where you go to take space. Something like, "If you are reading this message it means we got stirred up. I love you and care about you even though it doesn't feel like it right now. Very soon we will be connecting and laughing about how our nervous systems behave sometimes!"

Starting Where You Are

If reading this chapter feels overwhelming because you recognize yourself in the descriptions of hormonal depletion or having stupid fights with your loved ones, please be gentle with yourself. This isn't about adding pressure to fix everything at once. It's about understanding what's been happening so you can start making small, sustainable changes.

Maybe this week you focus on just one thing - perhaps the breathing technique we'll explore in Chapter 6, or incorporating one happiness hormone activity into your daily routine. Remember, your nervous system learned these patterns over time, and it will take time to establish new ones.

The most important thing to remember is this: your difficult emotions aren't character flaws or personal failings. Neither are you kids'. They're information about internal chemistry. When you can see depression, anxiety, irritability, or overwhelm as signs that your system needs support rather than evidence that something is wrong with you, you have just accomplished something profound. You can say, "A ha! there you are you pesky self-limiting belief! I am rewiring you right now!" Then breathe in to fullness, and out slowly to emptiness while soothing your nervous system. Smile broadly and say, "Ha ha ha" and chuckle. This is you rewiring on the spot. Excellent work!

You're not broken. You're not weak. You're not too sensitive. You're a human being whose nervous system has been doing its best to keep you safe, and now you're learning how to help it thrive.

In our next chapter, we'll explore how your brain coordinates this entire process, and why understanding the dance between your right and left brain can help you make sense of some of the most confusing aspects of trauma responses.

Exercise: Mapping Your Internal Medicine Cabinet

Reflect on your week. For one day, keep track of moments when you feel satisfied, joyful, connected, or simply "good"—and moments when you feel stressed, depleted, or overwhelmed. For each, jot down what you were doing, who you were with, and how your body felt at the time.

- **Happiness Chemicals:** When did you feel motivated, joyful, loving, or peaceful? Which activities or interactions brought these feelings?
- **Stress Chemicals:** When did you feel tense, anxious, or on edge? What was happening around you or inside your mind?
- **Noticing Patterns:** Are there certain routines or relationships that seem to "activate" your happiness or stress hormones?

Journal Prompts for Deeper Reflection

1. **Personal Chemistry Patterns:** What daily activities or people boost your "happy" chemistry? Which drain it? How does your body signal each?
2. **Stress Spiral:** Describe a recent situation when you felt your stress chemistry take over. What triggered it, and how did you respond?
3. **Celebrating Small Wins:** When did you last feel a "dopamine hit" (satisfaction after an accomplishment)? How can you create more of these moments?

4. **Connection Inventory:** Who helps you feel safe, loved, or calm (oxytocin moments)? How can you nurture these relationships?
5. **Body as Messenger:** When you view difficult emotions as chemistry, not character flaws, what shifts in your self-compassion?

3

The Dance of Your Brain

How the Right and Left Sides Work Together

Imagine your brain as a dance partnership. When the music is calm and everything is going well, both partners move in perfect harmony, each contributing their unique strengths to create something beautiful together. But when the music gets chaotic or threatening, one partner might suddenly take over, leaving the other unable to participate.

This is essentially what happens in your brain every day. Your right brain and left brain are designed to work together to help you navigate life, but trauma and stress can disrupt their partnership in ways that might leave you feeling confused, overwhelmed, or "not like yourself."

Understanding this dance has been one of the most helpful things I've learned in my decades of working with trauma, both in my own life and with my students. It explains so much about why we sometimes react in ways that surprise us, why logic doesn't always work when we're upset, and why healing requires more than just thinking our way through problems.

Meet Your Two-Part Brain

Let me introduce you to your brain's dance partners:

Your Right Brain is the keeper of emotions and memories. It's where your creativity, intuition, artistic sense, and your ability to see the big picture lives. It's nonverbal - it speaks in feelings, images, and sensations. Your right brain is also where your survival responses are coordinated. When you sense danger, your right brain is the one receiving and acting on the alarm. Your right brain manages your peripheral body so you can fight, flight or freeze depending on the situation.

Your Left Brain houses your logic and planning abilities. It's verbal, linear, and organized. It's where you form words, make sense of sequences, analyze situations, and plan for the future. Your left brain is like having a wise advisor who can help you think through problems and communicate your experience to others. Your left brain manages your rest and digest and perceives and interprets information from your vagus nerve. The vagus nerve is the longest nerve in the body and sends information from your brain to each organ, allows the organs to talk to each other, and scans the environment for safety. The vagus nerve is the part of your nervous system that sounds the danger alarm which alerts the right brain and the specific parts of your nervous system that controls your arms and legs to act.

When your vagus nerve senses safety, the right brain is at ease and you have access to all of your inherent gifts like creativity and happy feelings. It is able to team up with the left side, like the dance partners mentioned earlier, allowing fluid movement between logic and planning to work with creativity and artistry. We need both sides to get things done in life. When your vagus nerve senses danger of any kind, even low level indicators like frustration or worry, the gifts go dormant and the right brain's fight or flight mechanism turns on.

This is why consciously noticing your internal sensations and attending to them is essential for you to remain in direct connection with the positive gifts of both sides of your brain. When you do this, you can be who you are truly meant to be: a person with enthusiasm for life, doing what makes you happy and experiencing abundance in all the ways that matter, and not some frequently unhappy hot-head who is over-reacting to small setbacks or bumps in the road.

When you are in your green zone, the right and left brain are working well together, and you feel integrated. You can feel your emotions AND think clearly about them. You can access your creativity AND organize your thoughts. You can sense what's happening in your body AND put it into words.

But when they get disconnected - which is what happens during stress and trauma - things get complicated.

When the Dance Gets Disrupted

Let's go further into what happens when your right brain gets flooded. Your right brain, remember, is where emotions and survival responses live. When it receives the alarm signal - real or perceived based on past history - it can become so activated that it essentially drowns out your left brain's ability to function.

This is what Dr. Daniel Siegel calls a "right brain flood," and we've all experienced it. It's that moment when you're so upset that you literally can't find words. Someone says "just tell me what's wrong" and you want to, but you can't access language because language lives in your left brain, and your left brain has been overwhelmed by the emotional intensity from your right brain.

One of my students, Rachel, described this perfectly: "I can't find words. I bite and clench my jaw." That jaw clenching? That's her body's way of expressing what her left brain can't put into language at that moment.

This isn't a character flaw or a sign of immaturity. This is neurobiological reality. When your right brain floods, you literally lose access to what I call the "gifts of the brain" functions temporarily. The only way back is to let the flood recede, which is aided by the release of oxytocin, kindness, and the practice of the elongated exhale.

The Story of Perception and Interpretation

Earlier I mentioned that "perception" is the most important word in trauma work. Let me explain why through the lens of brain function.

Your Vagus nerve takes in emotional and sensory information, perception, while your left brain tries to make logical sense of it, interpretation. If danger is detected, and interpreted through cortisol, your right brain takes action. Together, they determine what's happening and whether you're safe or in danger. This team of perception and interpretation explain why we can watch a scary movie but know it isn't actually happening. Your heart rate will still increase, but your brain interprets that you are just sitting on the couch and not in actual danger.

But here's the crucial part: perception happens first and it is faster than light. You get an impulse and almost as fast, your brain decides how to interpret it based on your past experiences. If your early life taught your brain that certain situations are dangerous, your left brain will sound those same alarms and your right brain will carry it out, even when you're objectively safe now.

I shared earlier about growing up in a violent household where bickering led to dangerous escalations. Even now, when I hear people start to disagree, my left brain perceives danger and my right brain starts to flood with alarm signals. I now know how to use the skills in this book and redirect my nervous system back to my green zone. If you practice these skills, you will, too.

Right Brain Floods in Daily Life

Understanding right brain floods has been revolutionary for the families I work with. Instead of seeing emotional outbursts as manipulation or weakness, they can recognize them as neurobiological events that need support, not punishment.

When a child has what we typically call a "tantrum," what's actually happening is a right brain flood. Their emotional brain has become so activated that they've lost access to their logical, verbal brain. Telling them to "use your words" at that moment is like asking someone to write a thank-you note while their house is on fire. From this point forward, I want you to call anything that seems like a tantrum or meltdown a "right brain flood."

But here's what's beautiful: right brain floods don't last forever. They have a natural cycle, and if we can resist the urge to make them worse by getting activated ourselves, they will resolve. Like any flood, it recedes with time. Give your child and yourself loving, quiet space for each person's flood to recede. Then you can talk about what happened with the gifts of both sides of your brain ready and eager to reconnect.

One of my clients learned to respond to his teen's emotional overwhelm by saying lovingly, "I can see you're having really big feelings right now. When you're ready to talk, I'm here." Instead of demanding immediate compliance or trying to logic the child out of their feelings, he honored the neurobiological reality of what was happening. I cannot overemphasize the power of this tool!

If you say in a mocking tone, "I can see you are having big feelings right now" you will only be making things worse. You cannot give what you do not possess. If you are feeling manipulated or annoyed, it is better to say nothing. You are having your own right brain flood at the same time. Wait until you are better before attending to anyone else, to the best of your ability and as the situation allows.

Rewind: The Gifts Hidden in Each Side of the Brain

Getting yourself into your own green zone is the key. When your brain is working in integration, from your green zone, you have access to incredible gifts:

From your right brain: creativity, intuition, empathy, the ability to see patterns and connections, artistic expression, emotional intelligence, and the capacity for deep connection with others.

From your left brain: logical analysis, language and communication, planning and organization, problem-solving, and the ability to sequence and prioritize.

But here's what happens during chronic stress or trauma: cortisol (that stress hormone we talked about) actually interferes with the communication between your brain hemispheres. It's like static on a radio that makes it hard for your two brain halves to coordinate effectively.

This is why people who are chronically stressed often report feeling "scattered" or "not like themselves." They might lose access to their creativity, or find it hard to put their feelings into words, or struggle with planning and organization. They're not losing their intelligence or capabilities - they're experiencing the neurobiological effects of stress on brain integration.

The Breathing Bridge

Remember the elongated exhale breathing technique I mentioned earlier? Here's why it's so powerful from a brain perspective: that elongated exhale actually helps restore communication between your right and left brain.

When you're in a right-brain flood, intentional breathing helps calm the emotional activation enough that your left brain can come back online. It's like turning down the volume on the emotional alarm so your logical brain can contribute to the conversation again.

I had a student named Andrew who discovered this firsthand. He realized he was getting tense frequently - when waking the kids up, getting the baby ready to go somewhere, even getting her into her car seat. Why? Because the kids met him with tremendous resistance and whining. When he learned to notice that tension as an early warning sign and respond with breathing, he found he could stay integrated instead of moving into reactive mode.

"I noticed I have to take a step back and take a deep breath from some of the stressful situations," he shared. That step back wasn't avoidance - it was neurobiological wisdom. He was giving his brain the chance to stay integrated instead of moving into a survival response.

Things really changed for him when he started to understand that the kids were actually mirroring back **his** tension, not coming to him **with** tension. I asked him if the kids behave the same way when your wife does those things with them? The answer was "No." Light bulb! I pointed out that their vagus nerves were perceiving his anxiety and they were all going into the state of Caution with him and because of him! Once he understood that he radically changed his approach. The first thing he did was start getting ready earlier so he could attend to himself and start his day in his green zone. He also made sure there was time to be playful instead of rushing and it made the world of difference for all of them.

Working with Right-Brain Floods

When you or someone you love is experiencing a right-brain flood, here are some things that help:

Don't demand left-brain functions. This means no lecturing, no asking "why did you do that?", no insisting on verbal explanations at the moment.

Offer right-brain support. This might include safe physical presence or space, calm breathing, soothing tone of voice, or simply acknowledging the intensity of what they're experiencing.

Wait for the cycle to complete. Right-brain floods have a natural beginning, middle, and end. Trying to shortcut this process usually makes it last longer. Focus on you experiencing your own green zone, in their presence or nearby, and your loving, safe frequency will be the welcome home banner. When their flood recedes, they will come running back to you gladly.

Address it later when integration is restored. Once everyone is calm (including you, and most importantly, you) and you are both back in your green zones, THEN you can have conversations about what happened and what might help next time.

The Trauma Connection

For people who have experienced trauma, right-brain floods might happen more frequently and intensely than for others. This isn't weakness - it's adaptation. If your early experiences taught your right brain that the world is dangerous, it becomes hypervigilant, ready to sound alarms at the first sign of potential threat.

This hypervigilance was protective - it helped keep you safe in situations that truly were dangerous. But it can become problematic when your circumstances change but your brain's alarm system doesn't update accordingly.

Amanda, one of my students, had an insight about this when she analyzed her daily activities. She noticed that many of her stress responses were happening around child-related activities. Her right brain had learned to be hyperalert to the needs and emotions of others, which served her well as a caregiver but also meant she was frequently in low-level stress response mode, i.e. living in her yellow zone.

Understanding this helped her realize she wasn't "bad at parenting" - she was experiencing the effects of a sensitive nervous system that had learned to prioritize everyone else's safety and well-being, frequently at the expense of her own.

Building Integration

The goal isn't to suppress your right brain or override your emotions with logic. The goal is integration - helping your two brain hemispheres work together as a team.

Some activities that support brain integration:

Activate Oxytocin by saying, "Awwwwww" or "Ohhhhhhh" along with sipping water and sucking on some hard candy.

Breathing practices that involve slower and longer exhales, which engage left brain structure while calming right brain activation.

Mindful movement like stretching, shaking or walking, which engages both the physical/emotional right brain and the planning/organizing left brain.

Creative expression that includes singing, drumming, or playing an instrument or dancing or making art.

Storytelling about your experiences, which helps your left brain make meaning of right brain emotions and memories.

Co-Regulation and Brain Integration

Remember, you don't have to manage brain integration alone. In fact, one of the most powerful ways to restore integration is through co-regulation with someone who is integrated themselves.

When you're in a right brain flood and someone else stays calm and present with you, their integrated brain actually helps your brain remember how to come back into balance. This is why having someone say "Ohhhhhhhh, that sounds so hard" when you're upset can be more helpful than all the logical advice in the world.

This is especially important for parents and caregivers. When a child is in a right brain flood, your job isn't to fix it or make it go away, at least not initially. Your job is to stay integrated yourself so you can be a stabilizing presence that helps their nervous system remember how to calm down.

I believe this is the most important parenting skill there is and I hope it will become your parenting legacy: teaching your child how to self-soothe and get themselves back into their own green zones. This is one of those places where understanding and working with the science of our bodies is really handy. Believe me, kids of all ages, 5+, can do this work and they do! I have heard many stories about kids recognizing their parents' right brain floods and ask their parents, "Mom/

Dad, do you need some space? How about some breathing? You seem to be having some big feelings right now!"

The Long View

Please remember that brain integration is a practice, not a destination. You won't master this overnight, and you don't need to. The goal is developing awareness of when you're integrated versus when you're flooded, and having tools to gently support yourself back toward integration.

Some days you'll catch yourself early and be able to breathe your way back to balance quickly. Other days you might not realize you were flooded until hours later. Both are normal parts of the process, but more accurately, of being human.

What matters is that you're developing a different relationship with your own emotional and neurobiological responses. Instead of judging yourself for getting overwhelmed, you can recognize it as information about what your nervous system is dealing with and respond with compassion.

Your brain is not broken. Your emotional responses are not character flaws. You have a sophisticated neurobiological system that has been working to keep you safe, and now you're learning how to help it thrive.

In our next chapter, we'll dive deeper into the power of perception and how understanding this one concept can transform your relationship with stress, triggers, and healing.

Exercise: Right/Left Brain Awareness

Recall a recent time you were upset or overwhelmed. Note what happened in your body and mind:

- **Right Brain Flood:** Did you lose your words, get stuck in emotion, or feel "flooded"? What physical sensations accompanied this?

- **Integration Moments:** When you felt balanced and resourceful, what did that feel like in your body and thoughts? What helped you get there?
- **Support Strategies:** Try a creative activity (drawing, singing, or storytelling) and notice how your body and mood respond. Then try a logical activity (making a list, solving a puzzle) and notice the difference.

Journal Prompts for Deeper Reflection

1. **Flooding Signals:** What are your earliest signs of a right brain flood? How can you support yourself when you notice them?
2. **Integration Practices:** What activities or routines help your right and left brains work together? How do you feel afterward?
3. **Family Patterns:** Who in your family tends to operate from emotion, and who from logic? How does this show up in conflict?
4. **Words and Emotions:** Describe a time when you couldn't "use your words." What would compassion for your brain look like in that moment?
5. **Creative/Logical Balance:** How would your life change if you could access both creativity and logic more freely?

Part II: The Science of Feeling Safe

"Safety is not the absence of threat, it is the presence of connection."
— *Stephen Porges*

4

The Power of Perception

Why Perception Creates Your Reality

Of all the concepts I teach, the power of perception is the one that creates the most "aha" moments in my classes. It's the key that unlocks understanding about why two people can experience the exact same event or situation completely differently, why your stress responses sometimes seem to come out of nowhere, and why changing your circumstances doesn't always change how you feel.

Understanding perception has been personally transformative for me. For years, I carried the effects of growing up in a violent household without really understanding how it was still affecting me. I knew my childhood was difficult, but I thought I had "gotten over it." What I didn't realize was that my nervous system was still perceiving present-day situations through the lens of past danger.

The Slippery Thing That Drives Everything

Let me start with a story. In my classes, I often ask people to guess the most important word in trauma healing. It's written in capital letters in my materials, and there are usually a few words to choose from. People often guess words like "safety" or "healing" or "awareness."

But the most important word is "Interpretation."

Here's why: Your nervous system doesn't respond to what's actually happening at any given moment. It responds to how it perceives the situation and then interprets what's happening. And that interpretation is based heavily on your past experiences, particularly your earliest experiences when your nervous system was learning what the world was like for you. The thing is, over time we create deep beliefs about how life is, based on the average of our earliest experiences and feeling tones. We develop beliefs about how life is and operate from them until we notice them. Each person has their own beliefs, like "life is hard" or "life is easy." Say to yourself, "Life is _____." Fill in the blank over and over and see what you get. This will illuminate your predominant thoughts and beliefs about life.

This means you can be completely safe in the present moment, but if something in your current experience reminds your nervous system of a past danger, your body will flood with stress hormones as if that past danger is happening right now.

The Speed of Perception

Here's something crucial to understand: perception happens faster than conscious thought. Your nervous system is constantly scanning your environment and making split-second decisions about safety-caution-danger. This happens below the level of awareness, before your thinking brain even knows what's happening.

This is why you might suddenly feel anxious or upset without knowing why. Your nervous system has picked up on something - a tone of voice, a facial expression, an environmental cue - that reminds it of past danger, and it's already started the stress response before your conscious mind has figured out what triggered it.

One of my students, Roberta, had a beautiful insight about this. She realized that certain everyday situations were more stressful than she had consciously recognized. Her nervous system was picking up on cues that her thinking brain hadn't even noticed, creating low-level stress that she had been attributing to other causes. This frequently happened on her way to pick up her kids from school.

As a child, she frequently had to wait late after school for her mother to pick her up. Her mother was a drug addict and frequently slept during the day. Even though Roberta was not a drug addict, she fell into frequent worry about being late to pick up her kids. Even though she was rarely late, her experiences of the past welled up inside her. By the time she arrived, she was stressed out. She got in frequent fights with her kids for no apparent reason and pick-up became a chore for all of them. She thought they were just tired and cranky. It turned out they developed worry about seeing her and mirrored back her distress.

She went to her doctor for anxiety. It didn't really help her because the pills she received made her feel like a zombie. Her anti-anxiety meds actually made her feel more anxiety! I asked her about her physical internal sensations. At first she was perplexed by my question. It took her several *days* of slowing down and breathing while asking herself, "What are my internal physical sensations?" She identified, in a far-off way, a tightness in her chest, and that she feels it most intensely while driving to school to pick up her kids.

I asked her if that was a familiar feeling in her life, and to run the feeling backwards throughout her life and see if any memories popped up. By sitting with her chest discomfort and focusing on her elongated exhales in the current moment, she was able to recognize the same chest tightness when she would wait for her mother as a child.

This was a big "Aha!" moment for her. The action in the present brought up her experiences of the past, along with the discomfort that she felt then. This is how trauma works: the pain we endured gets encapsulated within our nervous system memory and just waits in perpetuity until we attend to them now. Think of where your couch is in your living room. You placed it there but it won't move unless you move it.

Our traumas have gravity just like the couch does. We have to notice where it is and then decide to move it. Sitting with our deepest discomfort takes courage. The steps aren't difficult, but they can be uncomfortable, depending on what actually happened and how you interpreted it.

With this deep understanding, Roberta stopped stressing and started looking forward to picking up her kids. She tested the mirroring system. She planned ahead, and watched to see what happened when she opened the car door while in her own green zone. Here kids were thrilled; there was no tension. She asked them what kind of treat they wanted and it became a wonderful part of their afternoons together. Instead of perpetuating the stress of her own pick-up experience, she was able to validate her childhood experiences, finally, and let them go. You can, too.

The Trauma Connection

If you've experienced trauma, your nervous system's perception and interpretation patterns were shaped by situations where hypervigilance actually kept you safe. Your brain learned to look for signs of danger because detecting those signs early was genuinely important for your survival.

This is adaptive learning - your nervous system was being smart, not pathological. The challenge comes when your circumstances change but your nervous system continues to operate from those same protective patterns (like in Roberta's example above.)

Looking for and attending to the strange patterns in your life, particularly where things do not go well on a regular basis, are the portals to your freedom. Warning: it takes courage, support and patience to sit with some of the darkest experiences you may have had. Just say, "God, please help me sit with this feeling." Breathe into fullness and slowly out to complete emptiness several times until you feel better. If you do not feel better, apply oxytocin by saying ,"Ahhhhh" or "Owwwww", sipping water and sucking on hard candy. Even if you do not feel better in the moment, assume any one of the steps you completed is working. Then put on some kickass music and sing along at the top of your lungs even if you still feel terrible. Keep breathing and focus on your elongated exhale. Depending on the severity of your right-brain flood, it might take some time to recover. Your right-brain flood **will** recede and you **will** feel better. This is the science of your body in action, working on your behalf.

Why This Matters for Healing

Understanding perception and interpretation changes how we approach healing. Instead of asking "Why am I being so sensitive?" or "Why can't I just get over this?", we can ask "What is my nervous system perceiving as dangerous right now, and does this interpretation fit my current reality?"

This shift from self-judgment to curiosity is profound. Curiosity is actually a green zone quality and instantly propels you into making happiness hormones, which is what you need to be able to say, "Adios" to your cortisol response.

Remember, you're not broken or weak if your nervous system interprets safety differently than others. You have a system that learned to be protective based on real experiences you lived through, even if you had what you thought was the perfect childhood. Your nervous system formed in the way it formed inside of you. It's personal and is your unique way of dealing with life. The details don't really matter. Your perceptions and interpretations do. Honor it, and it will honor you.

Jessica, one of my students who was feeling overwhelmed as a caregiver, had an important realization about interpretation. She began to understand that her frequent state of hypervigilance wasn't a character flaw - it was her nervous system's way of trying to stay on top of genuine challenges in her life. Her husband, Barry, on the other hand, was rarely bothered by the exact things that made her jumpy and nervous. By recognizing how his nervous system was perceiving and interpreting the exact same situations, she decided to borrow his interpretation, i.e. consciously co-regulate to his.

They agreed that he would say, "Hey, lovely lady, how about co-regulating with me?" It was cute and he would bat his eyes at her. That was their agreed upon cue for her to notice her internal commotion and slow her breathing down. At first she felt flustered because of her cortisol reaction. But soon she was able to laugh and that instantly changed her chemistry. She realized that not every moment required the high level of alertness she was prone to exhibiting. Her nervous system was interpreting many routine situations as emergencies when they were actually just normal parts of daily life.

The Generalization Effect

Here's another important aspect of how interpretation works: our nervous systems tend to generalize from specific experiences to broader categories. This is usually helpful - if touching a hot stove burns you, you are able to be cautious around all hot surfaces.

But trauma can also create generalizations that are too broad for current non-dangerous situations. If men with beards hurt you, your nervous system might interpret all men with beards as dangerous. If you had undiagnosed dyslexia you might have developed an aversion to being at school. If you got bitten by a dog when you were young, you may have developed a fear of dogs in general.

These generalizations made sense when they developed, but they might not serve you now. Therefore taking inventory of when you feel uneasy is an essential step in noticing when your nervous system goes into yellow or red zone chemistry production. This is especially important when caring for foster children or adopted children; their danger chemistry setting is often set at something really different from your family's setting. This is why it is important to see "tantrums" or weird behaviors as right brain floods, a nervous system response that happens due to trained perception and cannot be stopped once started. A good equivalent would be getting mad at someone having a seizure; pointless and cruel.

Working with Interpretation

The goal isn't to override your nervous system's interpretations or talk yourself out of them. Your nervous system's job is to keep you safe, and it takes that job very seriously. Trying to logic your way out of a stress response usually just creates more stress.

Instead, the goal is developing what I call "perception and interpretation awareness." This means noticing when your nervous system is activated and getting curious about what it might be responding to.

You might ask yourself:
- What is my nervous system picking up on right now?
- Does this remind me of something from my past?
- Is this interpretation fitting my current reality?
- What does my nervous system need to feel safer at this moment?

The Co-Regulation Factor

Remember, you don't have to work with perception and interpretation by yourself. One of the most powerful ways to help your nervous system update its interpretations is through co-regulation with people who feel safe to you. But here's the deal: sometimes the person who you would naturally go to is your spouse. This makes sense. However, often the relationship with a spouse is the longest relationship we have and the patterns of childhood beliefs get projected onto them inadvertently.

Here is an example from my marriage: my wife left the dinner dishes in the sink instead of putting them into the dishwasher. When I saw them in the morning, I had a yucky sinking feeling in my stomach (my perception of high caution) and I started to make cortisol. My brain interpreted my sinking feeling/cortisol as being abandoned and left on my own.

This happens at light speed. What used to come out of my mouth (also faster than logic) was, "Why are you so lazy?" As you can imagine, she didn't run over to do the dishes. I had to learn to insert a speed bump into my process: Short breaths in, followed by longer and longer exhales. I had to ask myself the questions I suggested earlier, most importantly, "Why am I having a cortisol flood about dishes?" I went to my wife and said, "Wow, I am having a terrible sinking feeling about the dishes." Notice me owning my cortisol experience. To which she replied, "Oh, I know. I was exhausted last night and forgot to finish them. Can you do them now, or do you want me to finish them?" Once I heard her say she forgot, and didn't leave them intentionally for me, treating me as a servant (which is where I go when I am having a right brain flood) I was happy to clean them.

When you're in a stress response and someone else stays calm and present, their nervous system can help you remember that the current situation is actually safe. This is why having someone say "Look around, You're safe, I'm here" can be more effective than trying to think your way out of a triggered state. Notice what happens when you reach out during your own stress response. If they run away screaming, you were probably blaming them for your internal experience. If they come to you, with compassion, you were owning your experience and they felt comfortable and were able to stay calm and present with you.

This is especially important in families where trauma is part of the history. Children's nervous systems are particularly sensitive to the interpretations of the adults around them. When caregivers can stay regulated during challenging moments, they help children's nervous systems learn new interpretations about safety and support.

Updating Your Internal Database

Think of your nervous system as having an internal database of experiences that it uses to interpret new situations. Trauma creates very vivid, emotionally charged entries in this database that your nervous system references when deciding how to respond to current experiences.

The beautiful thing is that this database can be updated. Every time you have an experience where something your nervous system interpreted as dangerous turns out to be safe, you're adding new data. Every time you successfully co-regulate with someone supportive during a stress response, you're teaching your nervous system that connection is possible even during difficult moments.

This updating process takes time and patience. Your nervous system won't abandon protective patterns that kept you safe until it has enough evidence that new patterns are reliable. This is wisdom, not resistance.

Environmental Factors

It's also important to recognize that interpretation isn't just about past trauma. Current environmental factors can absolutely influence how your nervous system interprets situations.

If you're living with ongoing stress - financial pressure, relationship conflicts, health challenges, caregiving demands - your nervous system's baseline level of alertness will be higher. This means situations that might normally feel manageable could be interpreted as threats simply because your system is already stretched thin.

This is why self-care isn't selfish - it's neurobiologically necessary. When you take care of your basic needs for rest, nutrition, connection, and stress management, you're helping your nervous system maintain more accurate interpretations of current reality.

The Ripple Effect

Understanding interpretation doesn't just help you - it helps everyone around you. When you can recognize that someone else's strong reaction might be their nervous system's interpretation of the situation rather than an accurate assessment of current danger, it changes how you respond to them.

Instead of getting defensive or trying to convince them they're wrong, you can offer the kind of co-regulation that helps nervous systems settle. You might say something like "I can see this feels really scary to you" or "Your nervous system is working hard to protect you right now."

This acknowledgment doesn't mean you agree with their interpretation - it means you understand that their nervous system is giving them real information based on their experience, even if that information doesn't match your experience of the same situation.

Practical Applications

Here are some ways to work with perception and interpretation in daily life:

Notice patterns: Start paying attention to situations that consistently activate your stress response. What might your nervous system be interpreting as dangerous in these moments?

Practice curious questioning: Instead of judging your responses, get curious about them. What past experience might this remind your nervous system of?

Communicate with your nervous system: You can actually talk to your nervous system like a friend. "I notice you're feeling scared right now. What are you picking up on? How can I help you feel safer?"

Create safety cues: Develop rituals or environmental cues that help your nervous system interpret current situations as safe. This might include certain music, scents, or comfort objects.

Seek support: Work with people who can help you stay regulated while you explore and update old interpretations.

The Long View

Remember, changing perception and interpretation patterns is not about erasing your past or pretending difficult things didn't happen. It's about honoring the wisdom your nervous system developed while also creating space for new experiences and new interpretations.

Your nervous system's protective perception and interpretations served you well when you needed them. Now, as your circumstances change, you can gently help your nervous system learn that there are new possibilities for safety and connection.

This is slow, patient work. Be gentle with yourself as you notice how perception and interpretation works in your own life. Every moment of awareness is a step toward greater freedom and choice in how you respond to life's challenges.

In our next chapter, we'll explore the nervous system map that helps you understand exactly where you are in any given moment and how to navigate back to safety and connection.

Exercise: Noticing Your Interpretations

Pick a recent situation where you felt triggered or misunderstood. Write down:

- **Initial Reaction:** What story did your nervous system tell you about what was happening?
- **Alternative Interpretations:** Can you list two or three other possible interpretations?
- **Body Response:** How did your interpretation affect your body and behavior?
- **Updating the Story:** If you could choose a new story or belief about the situation, what would it be?

Journal Prompts for Deeper Reflection

1. **Interpretation Origin:** What early experiences shaped your current interpretations of safety or danger?

2. **Pattern Tracking:** When was the last time two people had very different reactions to the same event? What did you learn?
3. **Curiosity Practice:** How can you use curiosity instead of judgment when you notice a strong reaction?
4. **Co-Regulation Role:** Who helps you reinterpret stressful moments, and how do they do it?
5. **New Possibilities:** Imagine responding to a common trigger with a new interpretation. How might that feel in your body?

Your Nervous System Map

Understanding Green, Yellow, and Red Zones

Imagine if your nervous system came with a GPS system that could tell you exactly where you were at any moment - not geographically, but emotionally and physiologically. A system that could say, "You are currently in the Anxiety Zone, moving toward Panic. Recalculating route to Safety Zone."

This isn't science fiction. You actually do have such a system, and learning to read it is one of the most life-changing tools you can possess. I call it your Nervous System Map. Whenever you find yourself lost in your emotional responses, you'll have your own personal map to help guide you back home to your green zone,

The Polyvagal Chart: Your Personal GPS

The map I use with my students is based on Dr. Stephen Porges' Polyvagal Theory, which explains how our nervous system evolved to keep us safe. I like to think of it as the history of our survival responses, written in our biology.

At the bottom is your **Green Zone** - this is your home base, your intended state of being. The driving force here is safety. When you're in your green zone, you feel calm, settled, grounded. You're curious and open, compassionate and mindful. You're present in your body and connected to the people around you. This is where your happiness hormones flow freely. This happy state of being is how you were designed to live, and this is your birthright! This book is about helping you claim your inheritance!

In the middle is your **Yellow Zone** - this is your caution/danger area. The driving force here is the perception of low to high caution. You might feel frustrated, worried, or concerned in the early yellow zone, moving toward irritation, anxiety, rage or panic as you go deeper. This is where stress hormones start to increase and the production of your happiness hormones stops.

At the top is your **Red Zone** - this is full survival mode when you are experiencing real or perceived high-level danger. The driving force here is the kind of danger that leads to life threat. In the red zone, you might experience a kind of freeze that is demonstrated through helplessness, numbness, depression, disassociation, shame or shutting down. Your body becomes flooded with high level stress hormones, and as I mentioned earlier, sometimes also makes certain happiness hormones like endorphins or serotonin to help you deal with the depth of threat you are experiencing.

The Water Metaphor

I like to think about this map using a water metaphor. Imagine your nervous system like water at different temperatures:

- **Green Zone** is like room temperature water - comfortable, sustainable, where you want to be most of the time

- **Yellow Zone** is like water heating up - simmering, getting warmer, moving toward a boil
- **Red Zone** is like water that's boiling and steaming, or frozen solid - extreme states that require immediate attention

Just like you can tell the difference between comfortable water and water that's too hot or too cold, you can learn to recognize what zone your nervous system is in based on how you feel in your body.

Your Personal Numbers

I use a number system with my students to make this even more concrete, from negative ten to positive ten. Negative ten is the deepest green zone possible, where you are in such a deep sleep that nothing could wake you up. Positive ten is the highest amount of stress you could possibly withstand before keeling over and dying. Nobody lives at a ten in either direction. While awake, a healthy state of being would be between negative three to positive three. This means you are alert and relaxed, highly functioning but able to laugh at whatever comes your way.

If you wake up at a negative two or negative three (feeling groggy, needing to hit snooze), and then you go through your morning routine - getting kids ready, dealing with traffic, dropping off at school - you might find yourself at a positive three or positive four in the yellow zone without even realizing it.

But if you wake up at a positive two or positive three (already feeling alert or even anxious), that same morning routine might push you to a positive seven or positive eight; dangerously into your red zone. Why do I mention this? Because really bad ideas seem like good ideas when we are out of our green zones. Red zone parenting is how kids end up in foster care.

This is why knowing your baseline is so important. Amanda, one of my students, realized through this mapping that she was starting most days already in her yellow zone. No wonder small challenges felt so overwhelming - she was already operating from cortisol before her day even began.

The Steps of Activation

Let me break down what this progression typically looks like when leaving the green zone:

Step 1: Frustration, Worry, Concern - This is your first step out of the green zone. You might notice tension in your body, changes in your breathing, or that familiar "off" feeling.

Step 2: Irritation, Anxiety - Things are ramping up. You might feel more agitated, have trouble concentrating, or notice your heart rate increasing.

Step 3: Anger, Fear - Now you're in more serious territory. Your stress hormones are definitely flowing, and your access to creativity and logical thinking is decreasing rapidly.

Step 4: Rage, Panic - This is deep yellow zone territory. Your nervous system is heading toward full survival mode. Logic is essentially offline, and you're operating purely from fight-or-flight instincts.

Step 5: Depression, Disassociation, Feeling Trapped, Freeze/Shutdown - When fight or flight doesn't resolve the perceived threat, your nervous system might drop into freeze mode - a kind of playing dead response that feels like complete shutdown or numbness. This is the red zone. Parenting and/or self-care decisions are at their worst from this location.

Individual Differences

One of the most important things to understand about this map is that people move through these zones differently. Some people are "fighters" - when they get activated, they tend to move toward anger and rage. Others are "flighters" - they move toward anxiety and panic. Still others tend toward the freeze response.

Rachel, one of my students, realized she tends toward the anxiety side. "I hold my breath when I'm anxious," she discovered. "I probably spend half my day holding my breath and don't even know it." This awareness became her early warning system - as soon as she noticed herself holding her breath, she knew she was moving into her yellow zone.

Andrew, another student, recognized himself more in the frustration to anger progression. He noticed he was getting tense frequently throughout the day, especially around child-related activities. Understanding this helped him catch himself earlier in the progression instead of waiting until he was fully activated and yelling at his kids. By the way, Andrew could not identify his internal physical sensations at first. The only thing he could really notice was the aftermath of yelling at someone. Only after a big explosion (of his) was he able to start to calm down and be able to feel anything internally. We backwards-mapped what happened for him. He found that he had a very quick experience of feeling trapped (high red zone) and that entrapment caused him to lash out quickly and harshly in an all-or-nothing way. This didn't make his family want to get close to him but just the opposite.

One of Andrew's chief complaints was that he felt isolated and that nobody loved him. We identified a tightening he had before he started to yell, a signal, his signal, of impending violence toward his family. During a session, he was able to isolate the tightness and remembered having the exact same feeling before his dad would yell at him. One day, soon after, when he was about to blow up at one of his kids, he yelled instead, "I'm feeling like I'm about to explode!" Then he ran into the bedroom and pulled the covers over his head.

An amazing thing happened: his family followed him into the bedroom. Curiosity, instead of fear, filled his family members. I remember him telling me how amazing it was when his son asked, "Daddy, are you alright?" At which point, he started to sob. His family just stood there, gripped with compassion for him. By owning his experience and not blaming anyone, they rallied together instead of operating in isolation. This was a pivotal moment for him and his family. Each person then started to notice and honor what they were feeling inside, and when they announced their internal physical sensations instead of saying someone was making them feel that way, curiosity, compassion and good old fashioned love was driving the self and co-regulation of their entire family. You and your family can do this, too.

The Co-Regulation Effect

Here's something fascinating about this map: we don't navigate it alone. Your nervous system is constantly syncing up with the nervous systems around you in a process called co-regulation.

If you're in your green zone at a negative one, and someone comes in at anxiety level (positive four), you might find yourself pulled up toward their level. But here's the beautiful thing: if you can stay grounded in your green zone, they're likely to come down toward your level instead.

This is why I teach people to become what I call "the regulator" rather than "the co-regulator." Ideally, the regulator is the person who maintains their green zone and helps others find their way back to safety. The co-regulator is the person who gets pulled into whatever zone the most activated person is in. Reminder: However has the strongest feeling tone frequency, positive or negative, is most often the regulator.

Practical Navigation

So how do you actually use this map in daily life? Here are some strategies:

Know Your Baseline: Pay attention to where you typically start your day. If you're waking up already in your yellow zone, you'll need to be more intentional about creating green zone experiences, starting with breathing yourself back to your green zone before you even get out of bed.

Notice Your Early Warning Signs: Everyone has different signals that they're moving out of their green zone. For some it's tension in the jaw, for others it's changes in their breathing, for others it's feeling "off" or agitated.

Have Zone-Appropriate Responses: If you're in low yellow zone (frustration, worry), breathing exercises and minor adjustments might be enough. If you're in red zone (depression, shut-down), you'll need more intensive support to get back to green.

Practice Zone Awareness with Others: Instead of just seeing someone as "difficult" or "overreacting," try to identify what zone they're in. Someone in the red zone can't access logic or verbal communication the same way someone in the green zone can.

The Breathing Bridge

Remember the elongated exhale breathing technique from earlier chapters? This is your most reliable tool for moving from any zone back toward green. The elongated exhale specifically tells your nervous system "we're safe enough to breathe slowly," which begins the process of turning off stress hormones and turning on happiness hormones.

But here's something important: if you're deep in your red zone, you might not be able to get to an elongated exhale right away. You might need to start with noticing your breathing and gradually work toward longer exhales as your system calms down.

Zone-Appropriate Expectations

One of the biggest mistakes I see people make is expecting green zone functioning from themselves or others when they're actually in yellow or red zones. You can't make complex decisions, access creativity, or communicate effectively when you're flooded with stress hormones.

This is why I teach people to avoid making important parenting decisions when they're in their yellow or red zones. As one of my students learned to say, "I need to get back to my green zone before we talk about this."

The Family Map

When you understand this mapping system, you can help your whole family navigate their zones more skillfully. Instead of punishing children for "tantrums," you can recognize when they're in their red zone and offer the kind of support that actually helps nervous systems calm down.

One of my clients learned to say to his child, "I can see you're having really big feelings right now. When you're ready to talk, I'm here." Instead of demanding immediate compliance, he honored where his child's nervous system was and offered co-regulation support. If you are the one who is upset, you can also say, "I can see I am having really big feelings right now. I can't talk now, so I am going to lay down and listen to some music for a while. Let's talk later."

Environmental Factors

Your zone isn't just determined by internal factors - your environment plays a huge role, too. Certain places, people, sounds, or smells might consistently push you toward your yellow or red zones. Other environments might naturally support your green zone.

Amanda discovered through her activity analysis worksheet (see chapter 7) that she felt most grounded and relaxed when doing animal chores or spending time in her garden. These became her go-to green zone activities when she noticed herself getting activated.

The Long View: Building Resilience

The goal isn't to never leave your green zone - that's not realistic or even healthy. Life presents genuine challenges that naturally activate our stress responses. The goal is to:

1. **Notice** when you're moving out of your green zone
2. **Apply** elongated exhale breathing technique
3. **Look** for what's triggering the activation
4. **Use Tools** to navigate back to your green zone

5. **Build Resilience** by practicing these skills, so your green becomes more stable over time

Think of it like physical fitness. The more you practice returning to your green zone, the stronger your "recovery muscles" become. Eventually, you might find that situations that used to send you deep into the red zone only push you into the yellow zone, and you return to green much more quickly.

Working with Trauma History

If you have a history of trauma, your nervous system map might look a little different. You might move through the zones more quickly, spend more time in yellow or red zones, or have a smaller green zone than others. This isn't wrong or broken - it's adaptive.

Your nervous system learned to be hypervigilant because there were real threats in your environment. Now, as your circumstances change, you can gently help your nervous system learn that there are new possibilities for safety.

This is patient work. Your nervous system won't abandon protective patterns until it has enough evidence that new patterns are reliable. Every time you successfully navigate back to your green zone, you're building that evidence.

Creating Your Personal Map

I encourage you to create your own version of this map. Notice:

- What does your green zone feel like in your body?
- What are your early warning signs that you're moving into the yellow zone?
- Do you tend toward fight, flight, or freeze when you get activated?
- What helps you return to the green zone most effectively?

- What environmental factors support or challenge your green zone?

This becomes your personal navigation system, as unique to you as your fingerprint.

Remember, this map isn't about judgment. There's nothing wrong with having yellow or red zone responses - they're part of being human. The power comes from awareness and choice. When you know where you are, you can make conscious decisions about where you want to go.

In our next chapter, we'll explore your most powerful tool for navigating this map: your breath, and how it can literally change your chemistry and guide you back to safety.

Exercise: Daily Zone Mapping

Over the next three days, pause three times a day to check your "zone."

- What physical sensations signal your current zone (green/yellow/red)?
- What events or thoughts triggered any shifts?
- What helped you return to green, if you did?
- Record patterns—times of day, environments, specific people.

Journal Prompts for Deeper Reflection

1. **Zone Baseline:** Where do you spend most of your time—green, yellow, or red? What influences this?
2. **Early Warning Signs:** What are your body's first cues that you're leaving your green zone?
3. **Family Map:** How do the zones of those you live or work with affect your own?

4. **Resilience Building:** When you return to green from yellow/red, what helps? How can you build more of these supports into your life?
5. **Environmental Influence:** What places or activities reliably help you shift zones?

6

The Breath as Medicine

Your Most Powerful Healing Tool

What if I told you that you already possess the most sophisticated healing tool ever created? That you carry it with you, every moment of every day, a technology more powerful than any medication, more reliable than any therapy technique, more accessible than any treatment modality?

You'd probably think I was exaggerating. But I'm not.

Your breath is the most direct path to regulating your nervous system, and learning to use it intentionally has changed more lives in my practice than any other single intervention. The breath is the bridge between your voluntary and involuntary nervous systems, the key that unlocks your body's natural healing capacity, and your most reliable tool for returning to safety when life feels overwhelming.

Why Breathing Works: The Science

Let me explain what happens in your body when you breathe in different ways. When you're stressed, anxious, or in survival mode, your breathing becomes shallow and rapid. This sends a signal to your nervous system that says "we're in danger" and triggers more stress hormone production.

But when you breathe slowly and deeply, especially with a long exhale, you activate what's called your parasympathetic nervous system - your rest and digest mode. The exhale specifically communicates with your vagus nerve telling it to relax, which is like a biological reset button that turns off stress hormone production and turns on happiness hormone production.

This isn't wishful thinking or new-age theory. This is basic human physiology. The vagus nerve, when activated by slow exhales, literally switches your brain chemistry from survive mode to thrive mode, where you are at your absolute best!

The 4-10 Breathing Technique

The specific technique I teach is what I call 4-10 breathing:

- Exhale deliberately with a whoosh and empty your lungs
- Flare your nostrils and breathe in through your nose for a count of four
- Breathe out through your mouth slowly (like you're blowing through a straw) for a count of ten
- Do this for several cycles, attempting to increase the length of your inhale and exhale, focusing predominantly on the exhale

To begin with, ten is the magic number to reach with your exhale. You may not be able to exhale to ten at first, but over time, you will be able to get there. That elongated exhale to the count of ten is a *scientific switch* that decreases stress hormone production and increases happiness hormone production. Ideally, try to breathe in for eight, and out for twenty.

Ultimately the numbers themselves do not matter. What matters is sighing and yawning, and elongated exhales, breathing into fullness and out to emptiness over and over, gently and slowly. Imagine a lion waking up from a nap, stretching and yawning. There is no danger, just the experience of being rejuvenated from resting. This is the kind of experience I want you to generate inside yourself consciously. By doing so, you will initiate happiness hormones and that is the chemistry of happiness and fulfillment in daily life, chores and all.

Here's the beauty about this: you don't have to set aside extra time to practice breathing. You're already breathing every moment of every day! You're going to breathe one way or another, so you might as well do it in a way that helps you thrive.

My First Breathing Lesson

Let me share what happened the first time I really experienced the power of intentional breathing. I was in a life-coaching session with my coach, Joan Menke. I was really worked up about something. She led me through the 4-10 breathing exercise, and asked me to really focus on my elongated exhales.

When we finished, the difference in how I felt was dramatic. Not just relaxed - actually restored. I felt like I had taken a 20-minute nap even though we had only been breathing for about five minutes. That's when I truly understood that this wasn't just a nice relaxation technique - this was actual medicine.

When You're Really Upset

Here's something important: when you're really activated - deep in your yellow or red zone - you might not be able to get to 4-10 breathing right away. And that's okay.

If you're really upset and you try my breathing technique and think, "This doesn't work," your nervous system needs more time to settle before it can access the longer counts.

You might need to hover at 2-5 breathing, or even 4-8, until your system calms down enough to extend the exhale. The key is the elongated exhale - however long you can manage in the moment.

Beyond the Counting

While I teach the 4-10 technique because having something to focus on can be helpful when you're upset, the real key is this: breathe into fullness through your nose, and breathe out to complete emptiness through your mouth, like you're blowing slowly through a straw.

It's that emptiness that triggers the vagus nerve response. You want to exhale until you have no more air to give, and then wait in that empty space for a moment before naturally inhaling again.

Sometimes when people are really activated, they can't focus on counting at all. In those moments, I tell them: "Just breathe out as slowly as you possibly can. Make it last as long as you can."

The Deflation Technique

During the exhale, I teach people to completely relax all their muscles - what I call "deflation." Imagine you're one of those inflatable dancing figures you see at car lots. During the exhale, let all the air out and become completely relaxed, like the dancing figure when the blower turns off.

This complete muscular relaxation during the exhale amplifies your nervous system reset. You're not just changing your breathing pattern - you're actively releasing physical tension and stress.

Breathing for Others

One of the most powerful applications of this technique is using it for co-regulation. When someone else is upset, instead of trying to calm them down with words, you can breathe yourself into *your own* green zone and become a regulating presence for them.

This is especially important for parents and caregivers. When a child is having a right-brain flood, your job isn't to make them stop crying. Your job is to breathe yourself into regulation so your calm nervous system can help their activated nervous system remember how to settle.

One of my clients learned to say, "Honey, you sound so upset. I'm going to breathe while you have your feelings, and when you're ready, I'm here." Instead of escalating the situation by getting activated himself, he became an anchor of safety.

Have you ever gone to your person in need of support and they got more upset than you were? This is a prime example of you being the upset emotional regulator and they co-regulated to your upset. This exact mechanism is why kids stop going to their parents when something upsetting happens.

The Acknowledgment and Acceptance Add-On

Here's an advanced technique that makes breathing even more powerful: combine it with acknowledgment and acceptance.

On the inhale, acknowledge what you're experiencing: "I acknowledge I'm feeling really tight in my chest right now."

On the exhale, accept what you are experiencing: "I accept that I'm feeling really tight in my chest right now."

This isn't about liking what you're experiencing or giving up on changing it. It's about stopping the additional stress that comes from fighting your own experience.

Working with Physical Sensations

Remember those physical sensations we talked about in Chapter 1? A good addition to acknowledging and accepting, is visualizing your physical internal sensations and working with them. This way, your breathing practice can be specifically tailored to address what you're experiencing.

If you notice tension, focus on blowing out that tension during your exhales. If you notice heaviness, imagine breathing lightness into your body and blowing out the heaviness. If you notice constriction, imagine your breath in creating space and expansion and your breath out blowing out the constriction.

Your breath becomes a conversation with your nervous system, a way of offering your body exactly what it needs in each moment.

Building Your Breathing Muscle

Like any skill, breathing regulation gets stronger with practice. I recommend what I call "maintenance breathing" - using the 4-10 technique during calm moments to build what I think of as your breathing muscle.

Practice at every stoplight, every time you go to the bathroom, once an hour during your workday. When you practice during calm moments, the technique becomes available to you during crisis moments.

Kerry, one of my students, developed a beautiful practice around this. She decided to do the breathing exercise every time she transitioned between activities during her day. This meant she was regularly returning to her green zone instead of letting stress accumulate throughout the day. You can do this, too.

When Breathing Feels Hard

Sometimes people tell me they don't like focusing on their breath, or that breathing exercises make them feel more anxious. This can happen for a few reasons:

If you've experienced trauma that involved breathing (choking, suffocation, panic attacks), paying attention to your breath might initially feel activating. Start very gently, maybe just noticing your natural breath without trying to change it.

If you have anxiety, you might be afraid that focusing on breathing will trigger a panic attack. Start with very short practices - maybe just three conscious breaths - and gradually build from there.

If you're very disconnected from your body, suddenly paying attention to breathing might feel overwhelming. This is normal, and it usually gets easier with gentle, consistent practice.

Breathing in Crisis

When you're in a full stress response - a right-brain flood - breathing becomes even more important, but you might need to modify your approach.

If someone is sobbing, don't try to get them to regulate their breathing immediately. Crying is actually one of the ways the body naturally washes away stress hormones; you can let that process complete while still being attentive. Once the intensity peaks, breathing can help with the recovery process.

You know this is really important, especially for men and boys. The "no-cry hammer" comes down in an awful way when males exhibit "weakness" by crying. Crying is the body's natural way to release cortisol. Cortisol build-up leads directly to rage and panic when it has nowhere safe to go. Just think about how our world would be if both men and women were encouraged to be honest about their internal experiences and were free to cry openly and unapologetically.

If someone is in a rage, breathing might not be accessible until they've moved some of the energy. Sometimes people need to stomp, shake their hands, or move their body before they can settle into breathing. Most importantly, the person needs to validate their own experience by saying, "I acknowledge I feel so _____ right now" on their inhale and, "I accept I feel so _____ right now" on their elongated exhales.

If someone is in freeze or shutdown, very gentle breathing - maybe just encouraging natural sighs - can help them begin to come back into their body. Invite them (or yourself) to lay down and place their right on their heart and their left hand on their tummy. Have them imagine an infinity loop or a figure "8" connecting loving feelings from their heart to their tummy and back, until they are able to breathe with elongated exhales.

The Ripple Effect

When you commit to using your breath as medicine, it doesn't just change you - it changes everyone around you. You become what I call a "regulating presence" for others. Another term I like is called, "being the emotional driver."

Think about an old fashioned stagecoach with four horses and a coach filled with people. The driver climbs to the top and sits in the front and when ready to depart picks up the reins and snaps them on the horses's backs and says, "Giddy up" or "Heeyah!" The sun is out and everything is fine, and the coach takes off. The horses are relaxed but working. The passengers sway to the rhythm of the horses' gait.

As long as the driver remains calm and steady, everyone, horses and people, are also calm and steady overall. I am not talking about kids fighting over a toy, I am talking about the overall understanding of safety. If something happens, like a band of robbers shows up or there is a need to flee a storm, the driver asserts a new dominance over the horses and passengers. The entire experience is now being fueled by danger and everyone's nervous system is co-regulating to that of the driver's; horses and people alike.

The question to ask is, "Who is your family's emotional driver most consistently?" This means, if we are all sitting around the house, pretty much doing okay, is there one person who frequently says, **"Heeyah!,"** and everyone goes into a tizzy, or frustration takes over the household, or everyone is suddenly tight?

Children are especially sensitive to the nervous system states of adults around them. You noticing your own internal state is the key to maintaining the positive emotional driver position. If your tension goes unnoticed in yourself, your family will still notice it in you and will either avoid you or react to how you really are even if you say and think you are fine.

When you're breathing yourself into regulation, your green zone, instead of getting activated by their emotions, you're teaching them that big feelings don't have to lead to big reactions. When you stop and say, "Wow, I notice I am having some big feelings right now," instead of yelling and telling everyone to go to their rooms, your honesty will create curiosity and compassion for you and for themselves. You will actually be the best emotional driver because you are owning your own internal experience instead of blaming someone for disrupting your internal experience and then making them responsible for yours.

At first this may seem really backwards, but it isn't. Every sentient being has to manage their own internal experiences. You demonstrating how to notice and then attend to your experience is the best way to teach others to do the same for themselves. This is the ultimate self-empowerment tool.

Partners, friends, and family members also respond to your regulated presence. When you can stay calm and breathe during conflicts or challenges, you create the possibility for everyone to approach the situation from their green zone instead of their red zone.

Your Breath as Your Best Friend

I want you to think of your breath as your best friend - someone who's always available, always supportive, always there when you need help. Your breath will never judge you, never abandon you, never require anything from you except the willingness to pay attention. When you breathe in, you are receiving the breath of life, just like you did when you were born. An abundance of oxygen makes happiness hormones. A deficit of oxygen makes stress hormones. It's as simple as that.

This FRIEND travels with you everywhere. No matter where you are or what's happening, you can always turn to your breath for support. It's the one tool that's never forgotten at home, never runs out of battery, and never breaks down.

There are numerous spiritual quotations about God, from many traditions, being in our very breath. That's how I like to think of it. When I am upset, I breathe God into my being. I look to God as my guide, meeting me in the green zone, my green zone. It is where we commune and is accessible anywhere I am, day or night. All I have to do is consciously exhale, emptying my lungs, and invite God in. God is right where **you** are, too, every minute of every day. Invite God in, right now!

Integration with Daily Life

The goal isn't to become someone who's constantly focused on breathing. The goal is to develop breath awareness - the ability to notice when your breathing is reflecting stress and to consciously use your breath to return to regulation.

You might notice you're holding your breath during a difficult conversation and choose to exhale slowly. You might catch yourself breathing rapidly before a challenging meeting and take a few 4-10 breaths to settle your nervous system. You might wake up feeling anxious and use breathing to start your day from your green zone instead of your yellow zone.

This becomes an ongoing conversation between you and your nervous system, mediated by your breath.

The Long Game

Remember, learning to use your breath as medicine is a practice, it's never "done" until you die. Some days you'll remember to breathe early in your stress response and easily return to calm. Other days you'll be deep in activation before you remember you have this tool. Both are normal.

What matters is that you're developing a different relationship with stress and overwhelm. Instead of being at the mercy of your nervous system's responses, you're learning to work with them skillfully.

Your breath is proof that you already have everything you need to begin healing. You do not need expensive equipment or specialized training or perfect circumstances to start. You just need the willingness to pay attention to something you're already doing every moment of every day.

In our next chapter, we'll explore how to apply this understanding in practical ways by becoming a detective of your own daily life, identifying exactly what supports your nervous system and what challenges it.

Exercise: Breath Awareness Journal
Pick one day to check in with your breathing at five random times.

- **Note:** Is it shallow or deep? Fast or slow?
- **Try:** 4-10 breathing or a slow, full exhale.
- **Record:** How your body and mind feel before and after.

Journal Prompts for Deeper Reflection
1. **Breath Patterns:** When do you notice your breath change during the day? What triggers this?
2. **Breathing as Ally:** How does it feel to imagine your breath as a friend or support?
3. **Crisis Moments:** Describe a time when conscious breathing helped you (or could have).
4. **Family Breath:** How could you introduce breath awareness to your family or children?
5. **Barriers:** What makes it hard to use your breath as a tool? How might you overcome these?

Part III: Practical Tools for Daily Life

"Self-care is not selfish. You cannot serve from an empty vessel."
— *Eleanor Brown*

7

Becoming Your Own Detective

The Activity Analysis Method

What if I told you that buried in your everyday routine are the keys to understanding why some days feel effortless while others feel like you're swimming upstream? That hidden in your normal activities are patterns that could explain why you feel energized after some interactions and drained after others?

This is exactly what my Activity Analysis Method helps you discover. It's like becoming a detective of your own life, gathering evidence about what truly supports your nervous system and what undermines it, often in ways you've never noticed before.

I developed this tool after working with countless clients who would say things like "I just feel terrible all the time but I don't know why" or "I love my kids but parenting feels so hard." The Activity Analysis Method helps you get specific about what's actually happening in your daily life and how it affects your internal chemistry.

The Story Behind the Tool

Let me tell you about John, a client who came to me completely burned out. He was a stay-at-home dad doing everything "right" - cooking healthy meals, taking kids to activities, maintaining the house - but he felt miserable most of the time and couldn't understand why.

When we did his activity analysis, fascinating patterns emerged. His morning routine of getting kids ready for school was giving him negative scores across the board. Not because he didn't love his children, but because one of his kids hated going to school and they battled every single morning.

But here's what was really interesting: driving to the first school was a negative six (our worst possible score and different from the green zone/red zone scoring), but driving to the second school was a positive three. Same dad, same car, same activity - completely different internal experience.

Why? Because after dropping off the child who struggled with school, he and his other son would get drive-thru coffee and have wonderful conversations. His nervous system went from being driven by one son, to being driven by the second son; his stress response went from entrapment to connection and joy in the span of thirty minutes, just by changing who was in the car with him.

This discovery was life-changing for John. He realized he wasn't a bad parent or weak person - he was having a normal nervous system response to starting every day with conflict. He also began to see how his sons were the emotional drivers so he started to make a plan for himself to remain the emotional driver no matter who was in the car with him. You can do this, too.

How the Analysis Works

The Activity Analysis Method is surprisingly simple (a link for this chart is found at the back of the book). You start by making a chart with your typical activities listed down the left side. Across the top, you write the physical sensations that represent your green zone (safety) and your yellow/red zones (caution/danger), two sensations for each prompt. Go see what you wrote for safe, confident, free, frustrated, afraid, and trapped, and write them at the top above each column, two for each as a starting point. You will have to practice with this and find the sensations that are your main indicators for you.

For each activity you listed, ask yourself: "When I do this activity, do I have this sensation?" Place an "X" in each box accordingly.

At the end of each row, you calculate a score: green zone experiences minus the combination of yellow and red zone experiences. This gives you a number that represents how that activity affects your nervous system.

Let me walk you through an example using John's scores, the dad I just described with two sons:

Wake up: He felt bubbly, energized, calm, peaceful, relaxed, and smiling. That's 6 green zone experiences and 0 yellow/red zone experiences = +6 score.

Think about getting kids ready: Immediately, tummy drop, feeling heavy. That's 0 green zone and 2 red zone experiences = -2 score.

Load kids in car: Nothing joyful about it. Multiple stress sensations activated = -6 score.

Drive to school #1: Battles with reluctant child = -5 score.

Drive to school #2: Peaceful time with cooperative child = +3 score.

This is the pattern I mentioned before. Same dad, same daily experience, but dramatically different nervous system responses to different parts of his routine.

Why does this matter? For John, taking his kids to school became a *habitually negative experience* that happened **EVERY DAY AT THE SAME TIME**. This means that all three of them were experiencing high levels of cortisol every day, together, at the beginning of their day. They all got used to it and just accepted it as how life is even though they hated it.

Once John saw that it was habitual and could be counted on happening, he realized he could plan ahead. He started a conversation with son #1 about his experience at school and brought his curiosity to him instead of his annoyance. Remember the story about my great-grandmother always kissing me on the ear? John started to really listen to his son and it turned out that his first class was in math, a subject that caused him great distress. John started to advocate better for his son and got him a first-period study hall where he could get help with his math. It's so easy to inadvertently squash the whiner. What you have to remember is that we only whine when we are uncomfortable. That discomfort is our nervous system telling us something is wrong.

My Personal Coffee Discovery

I have to share my own embarrassing discovery from doing this analysis. For months, I was having a terrible relationship with my French Press coffee maker every morning. I would stand in the kitchen, grinding beans, waiting for water to boil, getting increasingly irritated, and I couldn't figure out why mornings felt so hard. The fact is the grooves on the three-part filter were no longer working, so my filter would get stuck.

When I did my activity analysis, "make coffee" got a high negative score. I thought, "This is ridiculous! Honestly, who gets into a fight with their coffee? I'm teaching people about nervous system regulation and I'm getting stressed by my French Press!"

The solution was absurdly simple: I bought an automatic coffee maker with a timer. Now I wake up to the smell of fresh coffee, and my morning score went from negative six to positive six. Sometimes the answers are pleasantly practical.

Paula's Surprising Patterns

Paula, one of my students, had a profound experience with this analysis. She discovered that she had all high negative scores in the morning around her teen granddaughter. She also discovered something great: she felt really centered after she took her dog for a walk. Through this process she decided to let her teen get herself out of bed and ready for school while Paula took the dog out for a walk. Paula told her granddaughter, "You are totally capable of getting ready, I don't know why I was treating you like a baby. If you are ready by 7:50 I will take you to school. If not, here is a bus pass." At first it was rocky, but they both did better when they were each in charge of managing their own nervous systems.

I know some of you are shaking your heads emphatically right now thinking, "He will never go to to school if I do this!" That may be true. Some kids will respond well to being in charge of themselves and will rise to the occasion. Others will need more feedback from school authorities. The bottom line is you must maintain your own green zone for your own sanity. Demonstrate how to live well. Your child has to find their own way, anyway, no matter how much you try to help them. The more you are in your green zone, the easier it will be for them to talk with you about the predicaments they get themselves into; and that is the point of parenting.

The Four Key Questions

Once you've completed your initial analysis, examine each activity through four essential questions:

1. Is this necessary?

Sometimes we're burning through our nervous system resources on things that aren't actually required. Getting kids to school? Probably necessary. But battling them every morning about it? Maybe there's another way.

2. Is there another way to do this?

Maybe breakfast doesn't have to be a home-cooked meal if that creates stress. Maybe kids can make their own breakfast, or maybe you can prepare things the night before. Maybe getting everyone up 15 minutes earlier eliminates the rushing that creates conflict.

3. Is there someone else who can do this?

I worked with a former foster youth adult who was taking her kids to court-mandated video visits with their incarcerated fathers. This was giving her consistent negative scores because she had to interact with two men who had hurt her. When we asked question 3, she realized: "Oh my God! My mom can do this for me!" The visits still happened, but she didn't have to sacrifice her nervous system stability to make them happen.

4. Is there an attitude adjustment I can have?

Sometimes you're stuck with necessary activities that you can't delegate. But you might be able to change your relationship, i.e. your interpretation of them. I worked with a retired man who hated cleaning up after his dogs. When I asked about attitude adjustments, he realized he could look up at his beautiful ocean view while scooping poop instead of staying focused on the unpleasant task. Same activity, completely different internal experience.

Working with Family Patterns

One of the most powerful applications of this tool is doing it with your whole family. When everyone understands what activities support their nervous system and what activities challenge it, you can start making adjustments that help everyone thrive.

Rachel, one of my students, planned to "have my two teens do this so that I know what to look out for, and what time of day to be a little bit more careful or loving." This is brilliant - instead of being reactive to family stress, she was becoming proactive about preventing it.

The Complementary Partner Effect

Devorah, another student, had an insight about doing this analysis with her partner: "I think one of my biggest things is wanting to do this with my partner and see if there are some of these tasks that we are kind of complementary on."

This is beautiful. Sometimes what drains one partner energizes the other. Maybe you hate grocery shopping but your partner finds it relaxing. Maybe they hate doing laundry but you find it meditative.

When you understand each other's nervous system responses, you can divide responsibilities in ways that play to your strengths.

Beyond Individual Activities

As you get more sophisticated with this analysis, you can start looking at broader patterns:

Time of day: Do you consistently have better scores in the morning or evening? Are there certain times when your nervous system is more vulnerable?

Environmental factors: Do activities feel different when you're inside versus outside? In quiet versus noisy environments? Around certain people?

Seasonal patterns: Do your scores change with the weather, holidays, or school schedules?

Stress accumulation: How do your scores change throughout the day? Are you starting from a deficit, or does stress build up over time?

The Nervous System Budget

I like to think about this in terms of a "nervous system budget." You have a certain amount of resources available each day. Activities with positive scores add to your account, while activities with negative scores withdraw from it.

If you're starting the day in deficit (waking up already stressed) and then immediately engage in multiple negative-score activities, you're going to be overdrawn before lunch. But if you can frontload your day with some positive-score activities, you have more resilience for the challenging parts.

Making Sustainable Changes

The goal isn't to eliminate every negative-score activity from your life - that's not realistic. The goal is awareness and strategic adjustments.

Maybe you can't change the fact that getting kids ready for school is challenging, but you can:

- Prepare more things the night before to reduce morning stress
- Wake up 15 minutes earlier to eliminate rushing
- Play music that helps everyone feel calmer or energized
- Do some nervous system regulation (breathing) before engaging in the challenging activity

Working with Trauma History

If you have a history of trauma, your activity analysis might reveal that many routine activities create stress responses. This isn't your fault, and it doesn't mean you're broken. It means your nervous system learned to be protective in response to real dangers you experienced.

The beautiful thing about this awareness is that it removes shame and blame. Instead of thinking "Why am I so sensitive?" you can think "My nervous system is responding to something that reminds it of past danger. How can I help it feel safer in this situation?"

The Ripple Effect on Others

When you start making changes based on your activity analysis, it affects everyone around you. If you're less stressed during morning routines, your children start their day from a calmer place. If you're more intentional about including activities that restore you, you have more to give in your relationships.

Remember, you being in your green zone helps everyone else access their green zone. You taking care of your nervous system isn't selfish - it's the most generous thing you can do for the people you love.

Creating Your Weekly Practice

Based on your activity analysis, you can design what I call a "nervous system support practice." This might include:

- Starting each day with one green zone activity
- Taking nervous system breaks between challenging activities
- Ending each day with something that restores you
- Planning weekly activities that consistently support your well-being
- Identifying which days or times of week you need extra support

Common Discoveries

In my years of using this tool, I've noticed some common patterns:

The morning battle revelation: Many people discover that their entire day is negatively affected by stressful morning routines. Have a family meeting to brainstorm ways to make everyone's day start better. It may be that the child who hates school hates it for a good reason, one you should know about.

The people pattern: Certain relationships consistently drain energy while others consistently restore it. This phenomenon usually happens when both people are experiencing a cortisol response when interacting.

The environment effect: Activities that feel manageable in one setting feel overwhelming in another.

The preparation principle: A little advance preparation can completely change the nervous system impact of an activity.

The time-of-day factor: The same activity might be energizing in the morning and depleting in the evening, or vice versa.

Your Personal Experiment

I invite you to try this analysis for yourself. Start simple - just list 10-15 regular activities and notice how they affect your nervous system. You might be surprised by what you discover. Have your family do it as well. You will find some interesting patterns.

Remember, this isn't about judgment. There's nothing wrong with having activities that challenge your nervous system. The power comes from awareness and choice. When you know what affects you and how, you can make conscious decisions about how to structure your life in ways that support your well-being.

You are the expert on your own experience. This tool simply helps you access that expertise in a systematic way. Your nervous system has been giving you information all along - now you're learning to read it clearly.

In our next chapter, we'll take this understanding and create a practical, sustainable approach to supporting your happiness hormones throughout the week.

Exercise: Activity Scorecard

List 10 common daily activities. For each, rate on a scale from -5 (very draining) to +5 (very restorative):

- **Physical Sensations:** What does your body feel during/after?
- **Patterns:** Are there times of day, people, or places that make a difference?
- **Adjustments:** Pick one draining activity and brainstorm ways to modify, delegate, or reframe it.

Journal Prompts for Deeper Reflection
1. **Energy Leaks:** What everyday routines drain your energy most? Why?
2. **Restoration Rituals:** What small shifts could make daily life more supportive of your nervous system?
3. **Delegation Challenge:** What task could you let go of or share this week?
4. **Family Dynamics:** How do your routines interact with your family's stress or ease?
5. **Self-Compassion:** How does naming your energy patterns affect your self-judgment?

8

Creating Your Happiness Hormone Calendar

A Week of Intentional Healing

What if instead of randomly hoping good things would happen to you, you could intentionally design your week to support the exact brain chemistry you need to thrive? What if you could look at your calendar and know that you've built in specific activities to help your body produce the natural medicines that make life feel manageable and joyful?

This is exactly what the Happiness Hormone Calendar does. It's not about adding more to your already full life - it's about bringing intention to activities you can incorporate into your existing routine, but with awareness of how they affect your internal chemistry.

The Science Behind the Calendar

Remember our four happiness hormones: dopamine (satisfaction), endorphins (natural pain relief and mood boost), oxytocin (connection), and serotonin (feel-good baseline). Each of these hormones is produced in response to specific types of activities and experiences.

The beautiful thing is that you don't need to wait for these experiences to happen to you randomly. You can create the conditions for your body to produce these natural medicines intentionally.

I like to think of this like a weekly prescription for wellness, written by you, for you, based on what your nervous system actually needs.

Monday: Dopamine Day - The Achievement Hormone

Dopamine has the nickname "stressed mess" because when you're low in dopamine, that's exactly how people describe feeling: overwhelmed, unable to get things done, nothing feels satisfying.

Dopamine is released when you set goals and achieve them, when you experience satisfaction from completing something meaningful. The key is making your goals achievable. If you set huge goals and don't complete them, you actually get the opposite of dopamine - you get disappointment and discouragement.

Monday Dopamine Activities:
- Make a realistic to-do list and check things off
- Set small, achievable goals for the week
- Listen to music that makes you feel motivated
- Take a short walk while planning your day
- Complete one small task you've been putting off
- Organize one small area of your space
- Acknowledge something you accomplished recently

One of my clients discovered that his dopamine deficiency was connected to setting overwhelming goals. Instead of telling his son to "sit down and do all of your homework right now (which often led to overwhelm and shutdown), he started with "hey, let's set a timer for 15 minutes and then celebrate what you accomplished." In this way, he started training his son how to get steady hits of dopamine throughout his homework experience. This made it so much better for everyone.

The beauty of focusing on dopamine on Mondays is that it sets you up for a week of feeling capable and motivated. You're literally creating the brain chemistry that makes other activities feel more manageable.

Tuesday: Endorphin Day - Your Natural High

Endorphins are your body's natural morphine - "endo" meaning inside and "orphine" coming from morphine. These are your mood and pain regulators, your natural high, your body's way of creating feelings of joy and well-being.

Endorphins love intensity and they love group activities. You don't have to run a marathon to get endorphins - you just need to move your body in ways that feel intense for you, preferably with others.

Tuesday Endorphin Activities:
- Take a yoga class or do yoga videos
- Play a vigorous team sport
- Dance to music you love
- Take a brisk walk with a friend
- Play actively with children or pets
- Do any exercise that feels challenging for your current fitness level
- Laugh - watch something funny or spend time with people who make you laugh
- Eat a small amount of dark chocolate mindfully
- Get a massage or give yourself one

Kerry, one of my students, had a beautiful insight about endorphins when she mentioned doing yoga and exercise videos with her niece. That combination of movement and connection is endorphin gold.

The Tuesday focus on endorphins helps you recover from Monday's goal-oriented energy and prepares you for the social connection of Wednesday.

Wednesday: Cortisol Day – Lowering the Stress Hormone

Cortisol is your body's primary stress hormone, essential for survival but meant to be released only in short bursts. Chronic daily stress, even at low levels, keeps cortisol circulating and can leave you feeling wired, tired, anxious, or just "on edge." Over time, this wears down your body and spirit, making it harder to access joy, connection, and creativity.

Wednesday is your invitation to consciously step off the stress treadmill and give your nervous system a real break. This isn't about ignoring your responsibilities—it's about intentionally weaving in moments that signal to your body, "We're safe now. You can rest. You can heal."

How do you know you need a Cortisol Day?

If you notice you're rushing, easily irritated, reactive, or living with constant low-level tension, your stress hormones may be running the show. Even if you don't feel "stressed out," chronic busyness, overthinking, or an inability to relax are subtle signs your cortisol could use some attention.

Wednesday Cortisol-Lowering Activities:

- **Slow Down on Purpose:** Schedule a "pause" in your morning and afternoon—even 5 minutes—to simply breathe, stretch, or step outside. Let your body know it's safe to shift gears.
- **Connect with Your Senses:** Engage in activities that ground you in the present. Try sipping herbal tea, listening to calming music, noticing the scent of a candle, or feeling the texture of a soft blanket.

- **Nature Time:** Spend time outdoors, even briefly. Look at the sky, touch a leaf, listen to birds or water. Let nature's abundance remind you that you are part of a larger, supportive world.
- **Gentle Movement:** Choose restorative exercises—yoga, tai chi, slow walking, or stretching. The goal isn't to "work out," but to move in ways that soothe and reset your system.
- **Laughter & Lightness:** Watch a funny video, share a joke, or recall a favorite memory. Laughter signals your body to switch off cortisol and turn on relaxation chemistry.
- **Quality Time:** Be with someone who helps you feel comfortable and at ease. This could mean holding hands with a loved one, sharing a meal, or doing a mutually agreed-upon activity together.
- **Praise for Being, Not Doing:** Compliment yourself or others not for achievement, but for presence. Say, "I'm proud of you for getting through today," or, "Thank you for just being here with me."
- **Express Gratitude:** Jot down three things you're thankful for right now, no matter how small.
- **Restorative Ritual:** Take a warm bath, lie down with a weighted blanket, or read something inspiring before bed.

One of my clients created a "Wednesday Wind-Down" ritual: after work, she and her family would put away their phones, and sit in the living room together, listening to calming music before dinner. At first, the kids snickered, but soon it became everyone's favorite ritual.

Remember: You don't have to earn rest. Taking time to reset your stress chemistry is not indulgent—it's necessary for a thriving body, mind, and spirit.

The Power of Cortisol Reset

Choosing to lower cortisol midweek doesn't just make Wednesday easier—it pays dividends for the rest of your week. You'll likely notice more patience, clearer thinking, and a greater ability to enjoy the achievements and connections you build on other days.

You could even use Wednesday as a "midweek check-in." Ask yourself:

- Where is stress building up in my body?
- What would feel most soothing right now?
- How can I bring a bit more gentleness or slowness to the rest of my week?

A special affirmation for Cortisol Wednesdays:
High cortisol is often the Achilles heel of healing. Use this affirmation: "Even though I'm feeling stressed, I trust my body's natural ability to regulate and restore."

Thursday: Oxytocin Day - The Hug Hormone
Oxytocin is what I call "the Great Soother" hormone. When you release oxytocin, this soothing feeling flows through your brain and body like having the most loving, accepting parent you could imagine saying, "Oh, I love you so much. You're going to be okay."

The sound of oxytocin is "Awwww" or "Ohhhhhhhh." When someone is upset and you say "Ohhhhh, honey, that sounds so hard," you're not just offering sympathy - you're creating the conditions for oxytocin release in both of you.

Oxytocin Activities:
- Spend quality time with people you love
- Give or receive hugs (10-second hugs for maximum benefit)
- Have a meaningful conversation
- Care for pets or spend time with animals
- Do something nurturing for yourself or others
- Practice gratitude, especially for relationships
- Give someone a genuine compliment

- Write a note to someone you care about

Oxytocin is especially important if you've been feeling lonely or disconnected. You can be surrounded by people and still feel lonely if you're not producing enough oxytocin.

One of my clients discovered she was severely deficient in oxytocin. Even though she was surrounded by family who loved her, she felt profoundly lonely. Understanding this helped her recognize that she needed safe, wanted physical touch and quality time with others to feel truly connected.

Friday: Serotonin Day - Your Baseline Happiness

Serotonin is your feel-good hormone. When you have optimal serotonin, life feels good. You wake up thinking, "What a beautiful day!" You see the world through a lens of possibility and gratitude.

Serotonin is made in your gut, which is why you might get stomachaches when you're upset. It's also why positive thinking is so much easier when your serotonin levels are adequate - you literally have the brain chemistry to support optimistic thoughts.

Friday Serotonin Activities:
- Spend time in nature or sunlight
- Practice mindfulness or meditation
- Eat tryptophan-rich foods (turkey, eggs, nuts)
- Practice gratitude
- Do something creative that brings you joy
- Listen to music that makes you feel peaceful
- Take a warm bath
- Practice positive self-talk

If you've been struggling with negative thinking or pessimism, it isn't a character flaw - you might need serotonin. When serotonin is low, positive thinking becomes incredibly difficult because you don't have the brain chemistry to support optimistic thoughts.

Weekends: Integration, Rest and Restoration Days - Bringing It All Together

Weekends are for noticing how the week has gone and integrating what you've learned. This is when you celebrate what worked, adjust what didn't, and plan for sustainable practices going forward.

Integration Activities:
- Reflect on which activities felt most supportive this week
- Notice any changes in your mood, energy, or stress levels
- Plan which happiness hormone activities you want to continue
- Celebrate small wins from the week
- Connect with others about your experiences
- Prepare for a restful weekend

Weekend: Rest and Restoration

Weekends are for whatever your nervous system needs most - deeper rest, more intensive happiness hormone activities, or simply enjoying life without agenda.

Some people need structured weekend activities to feel good. Others need completely unstructured time. Pay attention to what actually restores you versus what you think should restore you.

Customizing Your Calendar

The beautiful thing about this approach is that it's completely customizable. You might discover that you need more dopamine and less oxytocin, or that endorphins are your go-to happiness hormone. You might find that certain days of the week are harder for you and need extra support.

Remember my student who discovered through her activity analysis that she felt most grounded when doing animal chores or spending time in her garden? These became her go-to activities when she needed to restore her nervous system. After a while, just walking outside made her feel better. Then, just the thought of gardening was enough to make her feel better. What are some things you love to do that make you feel calm and centered? Start thinking about them as soon as you get upset.

Starting Small

Please don't try to implement all of this at once. That's a recipe for overwhelm, which defeats the purpose entirely. Start with one day, or even one activity per day.

Maybe this week you just focus on setting one small achievable goal each Monday. Next week you might add a 10-minute walk on Tuesday. The following week you could add a gratitude practice on Thursday.

Remember, the goal is sustainable support for your nervous system, not another source of pressure or self-judgment.

Working with Resistance

Sometimes people resist this approach because it feels too structured or because they don't think they have time. Let me address both of these concerns:

"I don't like structure": This isn't about rigid scheduling. It's about awareness and intention. You might choose different activities each week, or you might focus more on weekends than weekdays. The structure is just a framework - you fill it in however works for you.

"I don't have time": Most of these activities can be incorporated into things you're already doing. Listening to music while you work (dopamine), taking the stairs instead of the elevator (endorphins), having a real conversation with your partner instead of just logistics (oxytocin), noticing something beautiful on your way to work (serotonin).

The Family Approach

One of the most powerful applications of this calendar is using it with your whole family. When everyone understands what supports their brain chemistry, you can plan family activities that work for multiple people.

Maybe Monday evening is when everyone shares their goals for the week. Tuesday could be family dance party or active play time. Wednesday might be family comedy night. Thursday might be one-on-one time with each child. Friday could be nature time or gratitude sharing.

Working with Deficits

If you take the happiness hormone assessment I mentioned earlier and discover you're particularly low in one hormone, you might want to focus extra attention on that area (please see Appendix A for information about taking the Tools for Life Happiness Hormones Quiz).

For example, if you're severely low in dopamine, you might include small goal-setting activities every day rather than just Mondays. If oxytocin is your biggest deficit, you might prioritize connection activities throughout the week.

Tracking Your Experience

I encourage people to notice how they feel before and after happiness hormone activities. You might notice:

- Changes in your mood or energy level
- Different responses to stress
- Improved sleep or appetite
- Better relationships with others
- Increased resilience during challenging times

Keep it simple - maybe just a quick check-in with yourself: "How do I feel right now compared to an hour ago?"

Seasonal Adjustments

Your happiness hormone needs might change with the seasons, your life circumstances, or your stress levels. In winter, you might need more serotonin support (light exposure, vitamin D). During busy periods, you might need extra dopamine support (smaller, more achievable goals). During times of grief or loss, you might need more oxytocin (connection and comfort).

Stay flexible and responsive to what your nervous system is telling you it needs. You'll know based on your physical internal sensations.

The Long Game

Remember, you're not trying to create "perfect" days or eliminate all stress from your life. You're building resilience - creating a foundation of nervous system support that helps you navigate whatever life brings.

Some weeks you'll follow your happiness hormone calendar beautifully and feel the benefits. Other weeks life will be too chaotic for structured self-care, and that's okay too. The awareness and tools you're developing will serve you in both kinds of weeks.

Making It Sustainable

The key to making this approach work long-term is finding the intersection between what your nervous system needs and what actually fits into your real life. This might take some experimentation.

Maybe yoga classes don't work for your schedule, but dancing in your kitchen while making dinner does. Maybe formal meditation feels too structured, but paying attention to your breathing during your commute works perfectly.

The best happiness hormone activity is the one you'll actually do consistently, not the one that sounds most impressive or "right."

Your brain chemistry matters. Your nervous system's needs matter. You taking care of yourself isn't selfish - it's essential. When you approach self-care from the perspective of supporting your actual neurobiology rather than following generic advice, you can sustain real changes in your everyday life experience.

You're not just going through the motions of wellness activities - you're engaging in precision medicine for your own nervous system, designed by you, for you, based on how your body works.

In our next chapter, we'll explore how this individual work translates into the beautiful dance of co-regulation, where your nervous system stability becomes a gift you offer to everyone around you.

Exercise: Weekly Wellness Prescription
Design a simple weekly plan:

- **Monday:** Dopamine (achievement)—one small goal
- **Tuesday:** Endorphins (movement/laughter)—one joyful activity
- **Wednesday:** Cortisol reset—one calming or nature activity
- **Thursday:** Oxytocin (connection)—one act of connection
- **Friday:** Serotonin (gratitude/peace)—one practice of appreciation
- **Weekend:** Integration—reflect and rest
  Track how each day's focus affects your mood and body.

Journal Prompts for Deeper Reflection
1. **Hormone Needs:** Which happiness hormone do you need most right now? What activities could support it?
2. **Intentional Self-Care:** How does it feel to plan for wellness instead of hoping for it?
3. **Family Involvement:** How could you invite others to join your weekly calendar?
4. **Barriers:** What gets in the way of following through? How might you adapt?
5. **Celebration:** What's one small win or joy you can celebrate from this week?

9

The Art of Co-Regulation

Healing Together

One of the most beautiful discoveries of my work with nervous systems is this: we don't heal alone. In fact, trying to heal in isolation often prolongs the very patterns we're trying to change. We are fundamentally social creatures, designed to regulate our nervous systems in relationship with others.

This process is called co-regulation, and understanding how it works has transformed not just my own relationships, but the relationships of every family I've had the privilege to work with.

What Co-Regulation Really Means

Co-regulation means that nervous systems naturally sync up with each other. When you're around someone who's calm and grounded, your nervous system tends to settle toward their state of regulation. When you're around someone who's anxious or activated, your nervous system might get pulled toward their activation.

This happens automatically, below the level of conscious awareness, through mechanisms we're only beginning to understand - things like matching breathing patterns, synchronizing heart rates, and picking up on subtle biochemical signals.

The crucial insight is this: someone is always the regulator or driver in any interaction. The question is whether you're choosing to be the regulator or unconsciously becoming the co-regulator.

The Story of Two Responses

Let me tell you about two different scenarios that illustrate the power of conscious co-regulation:

Scenario 1 - Unconscious Co-Regulation:
A child comes home from school clearly upset about something. The parent, seeing the child's distress, immediately *becomes anxious (i.e. co-regulating to the child's distress)* and asks, "What happened? Are you okay? Tell me right now what's wrong!" The parent's anxiety amplifies the child's upset, the child becomes more activated, which makes the parent more anxious, and soon everyone is in their red zone together.

Scenario 2 - Conscious Co-Regulation:
The same child comes home upset. The parent notices their own impulse to become anxious and instead takes several 4-10 breaths. The parent remains quiet but attentive and focuses on being in their own green zone. The parent says, "I can see something really upset you at school today. I'm going to sit right here and stay in my green zone. When you're ready to talk, I'm here." The parent's calm presence helps the child's nervous system settle, and soon they're able to share what happened from a more regulated place.

Same child, same problem, but completely different outcomes based on who became the regulator.

My Personal Co-Regulation Journey

I grew up in a violent household, where I learned about co-regulation in a scary and painful way. My nervous system learned to become hyper-vigilant the moment anyone around me became upset, which was frequently. Specifically, if I was upset about something, my parents got more upset. I didn't have anyone to help me get to my green zone. This created tremendous isolation for me in my family; I learned that going to my parents for support was not safe, and I avoided it whenever possible.

As an adult, this meant that whenever someone in my family was stressed out, I would become even more stressed about their stress. I perpetuated what I learned from my parents without realizing it. When my daughter was upset about something, I would become more upset than she was. I was unconsciously co-regulating to everyone else's nervous system states, which left me exhausted and everyone else feeling worse, not better.

Learning to become the regulator instead of the co-regulator changed everything. It meant developing the skills to stay in my green zone even when others were in their yellow or red zones, and offering that stability as a resource for others to return to calm.

The Polyvagal Understanding

Remember the Polyvagal Theory from Chapter 5? When you understand that people can be in different zones simultaneously, co-regulation makes perfect sense.

If you're in your green zone (feeling safe, grounded, connected) and someone comes to you in their yellow/red zone (frustrated, worried, anxious), there are two possibilities:

1. You join/mirror them in the yellow/red zone (unconscious co-regulation where they act as the regulator)
2. You help them settle back down into green zone with you (conscious co-regulation where you act as the regulator)

The person with the strongest nervous system regulation or dysregulation typically becomes the regulator for the interaction. What does this mean? The person with the highest intensity is likely to have the biggest influence on others. Unless you are aware of this dynamic and consciously choose to stay in your green zone, you might get sucked in. As soon as you notice what's going on inside of you, say "AHA!" and breathe yourself back to your own green zone. Then you will become the regulator on the spot.

Kerry's Insight About Not Chasing

Kerry, one of my students, had a beautiful insight about co-regulation when she said, "I love that you said don't chase to co-regulate, just be, and that will co-regulate."

This is so important. When someone is upset, our natural instinct is often to chase them with words, logic, or solutions. "Come on, calm down. Let me help you. Tell me what's wrong. It's going to be okay."

But chasing someone who's in their red zone often just makes them feel more overwhelmed. Instead, the most powerful thing you can do is breathe yourself into your green zone and simply be present. Your regulated nervous system becomes an invitation for their nervous system to settle.

Greg's Discovery About Breathing

Greg, another student, made a crucial connection when he realized he needed to "take a step back and take a deep breath" during stressful parenting moments. But as we worked together, he learned to refine this even further.

It's not just about taking a deep breath - it's about using that breath to return yourself to regulation so you can be helpful rather than adding to the activation in the room. When both parent and child are activated, nothing gets resolved and everyone feels worse.

The Foster Care Context

This understanding is especially crucial for foster and adoptive families. Children who have experienced trauma often come into new families with nervous systems that are stuck in survival mode. Their behavior might be testing, challenging, or confusing because their nervous system is interpreting the new environment through the lens of past danger.

Traditional discipline approaches often escalate these situations because they're based on the assumption that the child is making conscious choices to be difficult. But when you understand that their behavior is their nervous system's attempt to stay safe, that's when you can really help them heal.

One of my clients learned to say to his foster child, "I can see your nervous system is working really hard to protect you right now. You're safe here, and I'm going to stay calm while you have your big feelings."

The Language of Co-Regulation

The words you use during co-regulation matter, but your nervous system state matters more. A child's nervous system can detect whether you're truly calm or just pretending to be calm while feeling stressed inside.

Some phrases that support co-regulation:

- "I can see this is really hard for you"
- "Your feelings make sense"
- "I'm going to breathe while you have your feelings"
- "This feeling will pass"

Notice that none of these phrases try to fix, change, or logic away the person's experience. They simply acknowledge what's happening and offer presence.

When Co-Regulation Feels Hard

Sometimes people tell me they can't stay regulated when others are upset because it feels selfish or uncaring. They worry that staying calm means they don't care about the other person's pain.

But the opposite is true. When you can stay regulated during someone else's crisis, you're offering them the greatest gift possible - a nervous system anchor that can help them find their way back to safety in themselves!

This doesn't mean being cold or detached. It means caring so much that you're willing to do the hard work of managing your own nervous system so you can be truly helpful. This means you aren't trying to fix them but you accept them as they are. Doing this will almost guarantee that your people will come to you when they need help.

Rachel and Andrew's Team Approach

Rachel mentioned in class that because her husband, Andrew, was also participating in the training, they were planning to share their activity analyses with each other. This is brilliant co-regulation work.

When partners understand each other's nervous system patterns - what activates them, what calms them, what time of day they're most vulnerable - they can support each other more effectively. Instead of taking each other's stress responses personally, they can recognize when someone needs co-regulation support.

The Breathing Connection

Remember the 4-10 breathing technique from Chapter 6? This becomes especially powerful in co-regulation situations. When someone you love is upset, instead of trying to calm them down with words, you can breathe yourself into regulation and let your calm nervous system do the co-regulating.

Children are especially responsive to this. They might not be able to consciously breathe when they're upset, but they will unconsciously begin to match your breathing pattern as their nervous system settles toward yours, even if you are in another room!

Co-Regulation vs. Co-dependence

It's important to distinguish between healthy co-regulation and co-dependence. In co-regulation, you maintain your own nervous system stability while offering support to others. In co-dependence, you lose yourself in others' emotional states and try to control their experiences.

Healthy co-regulation looks like:

- Staying grounded in your own green zone while others are activated
- Offering presence without trying to fix or change others
- Maintaining appropriate boundaries about what you can and cannot control
- Taking care of your own nervous system needs so you can be available to others

Working with Trauma Triggers

When someone has a trauma history, certain situations might trigger intense nervous system responses that seem disproportionate to current circumstances. Understanding co-regulation helps you respond to these moments more effectively.

A typical response might be to brush it off - by saying "That was a long time ago, it shouldn't still bother you" or "Why are you still upset about that, you're safe now."

Instead, say something that acknowledges what they are experiencing in the moment, like, " I can see that you're really upset right now," or, "I hear you're not feeling safe right now."

Instead of attempting to engage their logical brain when they're in emotional overwhelm i.e. having a right-brain flood, acknowledge their experience. This offers nervous system co-regulation through your presence, breathing, and calm tone of voice.

The Family System Approach

Co-regulation works best when the whole family understands how nervous systems work. This might mean having family meetings about everyone's stress signals, creating family breathing practices, or establishing agreements about how to support each other during difficult moments.

One family I worked with created a simple system: when anyone noticed they were moving into their yellow or red zone, they would say "I need a regulation break" and take 5 minutes to breathe. Family members learned not to chase or pressure during these breaks, and to offer welcome-back hugs when the person returned.

The Ripple Effect of Regulation

When you become skilled at co-regulation, it doesn't just help your immediate family - it affects every interaction you have. You become a "regulating presence" in your world.

Your calm in the grocery store checkout line might help a stressed cashier settle. Your groundedness during a tense meeting might help colleagues think more clearly. Your peace during a neighborhood conflict might help others find solutions rather than escalate problems.

Building Co-Regulation Skills

Co-regulation is a learnable skill that gets stronger with practice. Some ways to develop it:

Practice regulating yourself first: You can't offer others what you don't have. Develop your own nervous system awareness and regulation skills before trying to help others.

Start with calm moments: Practice co-regulation during ordinary interactions when no one is upset. This builds the skill so it's available during crisis moments.

Notice your patterns: Pay attention to which people or situations tend to dysregulate you, and practice staying grounded in those contexts.

Use your breath: Remember that your breathing pattern affects others unconsciously. Slow, deep breathing invites others to breathe more calmly too.

Trust the process: Co-regulation takes time. Don't expect immediate results, especially with people who have trauma histories or chronic stress patterns.

When Professional Help is Needed

While co-regulation is powerful, it's not a substitute for professional mental health support when needed. If someone's nervous system dysregulation is severe, persistent, or interfering with daily functioning, additional help may be necessary.

Co-regulation works best as part of a comprehensive approach to healing that might include therapy, medical support, and other interventions as appropriate.

The Long View of Healing

Remember that learning co-regulation, but more importantly, self-regulation, is a practice, not a perfection. Because you are alive, your nervous system has to work for you every day, it doesn't go on vacation. Therefore, you have to manage it every day. If you ignore your nervous system, and its cues, you may find yourself with illnesses and diagnoses that you probably won't enjoy having.

Unless you are born with a congenital disease, the vast majority of chronic problems start as your dashboard alerting you to something you are perceiving as dangerous. The longer you ignore the cues, the longer it will take to undo them. It's just like a ball of yarn that was haphazardly rolled up; there are knots and snarls and some of them will be tight. It takes patience to unwind a human being!

You'll have days when you successfully stay regulated during family chaos and feel amazed at the difference it makes. You'll also have days when everyone's activation triggers your activation and you all end up in the red zone together.

Both experiences are part of the learning process. What matters is developing awareness of how co-regulation works and having tools to return to it when you get off track.

The goal isn't to become someone who never gets activated - that's not realistic or even healthy. The goal is to become someone who can recognize when you're activated, take responsibility for your own regulation (which actually means taking responsibility for your dysregulation), and offer your stability as a resource for others when they need it.

This is how families heal. This is how communities heal. This is how we break generational patterns of trauma and create new patterns of safety and connection.

Exercise: Co-Regulation Inventory
Think back on the past week.

- Who helps you feel calmer or more grounded?
- When did you notice yourself syncing up (positively or negatively) with another's mood?
- What did you do, or what could you do, to be the "regulator" in those moments?
- Try practicing slow breathing with someone and share your experience.

Journal Prompts for Deeper Reflection
1. **Regulator or Co-Regulator:** In stressful situations, do you tend to anchor others or get swept up in their states?
2. **Relationship Patterns:** How does your mood affect those around you? How do theirs affect you?

3. **Support Signals:** What cues could you use with loved ones when you need a break or support?
4. **Learning Together:** What would it look like to make co-regulation a family or partnership skill?
5. **Healing in Community:** How does the idea that "we heal together" resonate with your own experience?

Part IV: Breaking Generational Patterns

"The most important thing we can do is interrupt the intergenerational transmission of trauma, not by hiding from it, but by owning our story and walking through it."
—Brené Brown

10

When the Past Lives in Your Body

Understanding Trauma's Legacy

There's something I need you to understand about trauma: trauma isn't what happened to you. Trauma is what happens inside you as a result of what happened to you. More specifically, trauma lives in your body as stored sensations, memories, and protective patterns that continue to influence how you move through the world long after the original events have ended.

Your body is an exquisite recording device. Every significant experience - especially those that involved fear, pain, or overwhelm - gets encoded not just in your mind, but in your muscles, your breathing patterns, your posture, your nervous system responses. These body memories don't fade with time the way conscious memories do. They remain alive and active, ready to protect you from similar threats, even when those threats no longer exist.

Understanding this changes how we approach healing. It's not enough to think our way through trauma - we need to work with the body where these memories are stored. This isn't about reliving painful experiences, but about gently helping your nervous system update its protective patterns to match your current reality.

When Safety Feels Dangerous: A Key Discovery

Remember back in Chapter 1 when I asked you to do the Quick Write Exercise? I had you say "I am safe" and notice what physical sensations came up in your body. If you're like many people who have experienced trauma, something surprising might have happened: instead of feeling good sensations when you said "I am safe," you might have felt something uncomfortable - tightness, anxiety, or even panic.

If this happened to you, this chapter is especially for you. You're not broken. You've just discovered something profound about how your nervous system learned to survive. For some people, especially those with trauma histories, the idea of safety itself can feel dangerous because it means letting your guard down - and letting your guard down in the past might have led to getting hurt.

This is exactly the kind of pattern that needs gentle updating. This is how a person may end up living in their Yellow and Red zones, without even knowing it. Your nervous system learned these responses for good reasons, but now they might be keeping you from experiencing the peace and connection you deserve.

Updating Your Safety Templates

If you had negative reactions to the words "safe," "confident," or "free" in Chapter 1, here's how you can begin to update your nervous system's templates. Instead of fighting against the uncomfortable sensations, we're going to help your nervous system remember what safety could feel like.

Try this gentle exercise:

Ask yourself: "If I were to feel safe, I imagine I would experience the following internal physical sensations_____."

Don't worry about what you actually feel right now. Just imagine what safety might feel like in your body. Maybe it would feel like warm relaxation, like your shoulders dropping, like breathing easily, like a sense of lightness or expansion.

Then: "If I were to feel confident, I would experience the following internal physical sensations_____."

Again, imagine what confidence might feel like - perhaps a sense of groundedness, an upright posture, a feeling of strength or capability.

Finally: "If I were to feel free, I would experience the following internal physical sensations_____."

What would freedom feel like in your body? Maybe like spaciousness, like the ability to move easily, like lightness or joy.

There are no wrong answers here - you're teaching your nervous system new possibilities.

Now, let's take this a step further. Think of a recent time when you were in conflict with someone and you had a big reaction - maybe you got angry, shut down, or felt overwhelmed. In recalling that moment, ask yourself:

"If I had felt safe during that conflict, what kind of internal physical sensation would I have felt?" Maybe you would have felt grounded, steady, able to breathe easily even while discussing difficult things.

"If I had felt confident during that conflict, what would that have felt like in my body?" Perhaps you would have felt solid in yourself, able to speak clearly, not threatened by the other person's emotions.

"If I had felt free during that conflict, what physical sensations would I have experienced?" Maybe you would have felt at choice and flexible, able to choose your response rather than react automatically.

You're not trying to change the past or judge your reactions. You're giving your nervous system new information about what's possible. Without giving the possibility of a different or new outcome, your nervous system stays stuck in the same loop it's always been on. Just imagining a new outcome is enough to begin updating it's database and start to magnetize you to your new desired outcome. The more you imagine the new outcome and experience those sensations in your body, the stronger the new neural pathway. As I mentioned earlier, our nervous system needs to have a great amount of proof that something works before it will discard an old pattern. Every time you imagine it, and then have little bits of it shining through in your communications, your proving to your nervous system that another outcome is possible.

The Body's Memory System

Your body remembers everything in a language that has nothing to do with words. When you were a baby and someone held you close, patting your back gently while making soothing sounds like "Awwww," your nervous system learned that rhythmic touch and soft sounds mean safety and comfort. This is why when babies are fussy, we instinctively rock them, pat their backs, and make those gentle "awwww" sounds - we're speaking directly to their nervous system in the ancient language of safety.

What's remarkable is that making the sound "awwww" actually releases oxytocin - that powerful "love and connection" hormone - in both you and the person you're comforting. It's like a biological reset button that tells both nervous systems, "You're safe, you're loved, everything is going to be okay."

The Self-Soothing Touch: Learning From How We Comfort Babies

Just like comforting a baby with gentle patting and soothing sounds, you can use these same techniques on yourself. When you're feeling overwhelmed or activated, you can place your hands on your heart or stomach and gently pat or rub in circular motions while making that soft "awwww" sound.

This isn't childish or silly - it's profound nervous system medicine. You're literally speaking to your body in the language it learned before you could even talk, telling it that you're safe and cared for. The combination of gentle touch and the "awwww" sound releases oxytocin, which helps calm your entire system.

The Science of Rhythmic Touch: Tapping and EFT

The power of rhythmic touch to regulate the nervous system has been formalized in various therapeutic approaches. One powerful approach is Emotional Freedom Technique (EFT), also known as meridian tapping or simply "tapping." While EFT involves specific protocols and acupressure points, the underlying principle is beautifully simple: rhythmic tapping on the body sends safety signals to the nervous system.

Just like that elongated exhale we've practiced, gentle tapping acts as a biological switch that tells your nervous system you're safe. The rhythmic nature of the touch mimics the comforting patterns we experienced as babies - the patting on the back, the gentle rocking, the steady heartbeat we heard in the womb.

You don't need to learn complex tapping protocols to benefit from this principle. Simply tapping gently on your chest, your arms, or your legs while breathing slowly can help activate your parasympathetic nervous system and move you back toward your green zone. When I combine the tapping with the soft "awwww" sound and slow breathing, I create what I think of as a "triple soothing system" - touch, sound, and breath all working together to tell my nervous system that everything is okay.

The Adaptive Nature of Trauma Responses

One of the most important shifts in understanding trauma is recognizing that trauma responses were adaptive. Your nervous system wasn't broken or damaged by difficult experiences - it was learning how to survive them.

If you learned to be hypervigilant because your environment truly was unpredictable, that hypervigilance served you well. If you learned to shut down emotionally because expressing feelings wasn't safe, that shutdown protected you. These patterns deserve respect, not judgment. They represent your body's fierce commitment to your survival.

The challenge comes when your circumstances change but your nervous system continues operating from those same protective patterns.

Understanding Triggers as Body Memory Activators

What we call "triggers" are really just reminders that activate stored body memories. A trigger doesn't have to be obviously connected to the original trauma - sometimes it's something as simple as a particular quality of light, a tone of voice, or the way someone moves their hands that suddenly transports your nervous system back to an old state of alarm.

Understanding triggers from a body memory perspective removes the shame and self-judgment that often accompany them. You're not being "too sensitive" or "overreacting." Your body is doing exactly what it was designed to do - recognize patterns that once spelled danger and prepare you to respond.

The key is learning to recognize when you're experiencing a body memory rather than responding to a current threat. This awareness creates a crucial pause between trigger and reaction, a space where choice becomes possible. Sometimes this is easy to do, others, not so much.

Creating New Body Memories of Safety

While we can't erase difficult body memories, we can create new ones that provide your nervous system with updated information about safety and support. Every time you successfully navigate a challenging situation while staying in your green zone, you're creating new body memories of resilience and competence.

Every time you use gentle touch, soothing sounds, and conscious breathing to comfort yourself when you're distressed, you're creating body memories that you can be a source of safety for yourself. When you practice those "If I felt safe, I would feel..." exercises, you're literally teaching your nervous system what safety could feel like in this moment.

Practice creating positive body memories intentionally. When you're in your green zone, really feel it while placing gentle hands on yourself and making those soothing sounds. Notice how safety feels in your muscles, your breathing, your posture when combined with nurturing touch and sound. This practice literally stores up these sensations like money in the bank - they become resources you can draw on during challenging times.

The Daily Practice of Body-Based Healing

Working with body memories isn't something you do only during crisis moments. It's most effective as a gentle, daily practice that helps your nervous system gradually update its protective patterns.

Start each day with a brief body check-in. Where are you on the number line we discussed earlier? Place your hands on your heart and stomach, do some gentle tapping, and take three slow breaths while asking yourself, "If I felt safe in my body right now, what would that feel like?" End each day the same way, offering your body gratitude for carrying you through another day while giving it some comfort through touch and sound.

Throughout the day, when you notice stress beginning to build, pause and offer your body the same comfort you would give to an upset child. Place a gentle hand on your chest, do some soft tapping, take slow breaths, and make soft "awwww" sounds. This isn't indulgent - it's preventive medicine for your nervous system.

The Ripple Effect of Your Healing

Here's something beautiful about healing your own trauma patterns: it doesn't just help you. Every time you choose to breathe instead of react, respond to someone else's activation with regulation instead of escalation, or break a pattern that was passed down to you, you're changing the trajectory for future generations.

The people in your life are watching and learning from how you handle stress, emotions, and relationships. When they see you pause to regulate yourself instead of acting from overwhelm, they're learning that this is possible for them, too.

Professional Support for Body-Based Healing

While the tools in this book can be incredibly helpful for working with body memories, sometimes professional support is necessary, especially for severe or complex trauma. Somatic therapists, EFT practitioners, body workers who understand trauma, and other professionals trained in body-based healing can provide specialized support for this work.

The nervous system regulation skills you're learning here can complement and enhance professional treatment, but they're not necessarily a substitute for it when deeper healing work is needed.

Your Body as Your Guide

As we work toward healing, I want you to begin seeing your body as your greatest ally rather than your enemy. Yes, it might react to situations in ways that feel inconvenient. Yes, it might carry painful memories. But it has also carried you through every challenge you've faced, adapted to protect you in whatever ways it could, and continues to work tirelessly on your behalf.

Your body's sensitivity isn't a flaw - it's evidence of its intelligence. Your body's protective patterns aren't obstacles - they're proof of its dedication to your survival. When you can approach your body with the same gentleness you would show a frightened child, when you can offer it the same comfort you would give to someone you love dearly, you create the conditions for genuine healing to occur.

Remember, you carry within your very cells the memory of every time you were comforted, every moment you felt safe, every experience of love and tenderness. These positive body memories are there too, waiting to be awakened by your own gentle touch and conscious care.

Your body has been waiting patiently for you to return to it with kindness. When you begin to work with your body as a partner in healing rather than an obstacle to overcome, everything changes.

Exercise: Body Memory Exploration and Updating

Safety Template Updating: If you had negative reactions to "safe," "confident," or "free" in Chapter 1, practice the updating exercise. Complete these sentences: "If I felt safe, I would feel _____." "If I felt confident, I would feel _____." "If I felt free, I would feel _____."

Conflict Reframing: Think of a recent conflict where you had a big reaction. Ask yourself: "If I had felt safe during that conflict, what physical sensations would I have experienced?" Repeat for confident and free.

Self-Soothing Practice: Place one hand on your heart and one on your stomach. Do gentle tapping while making soft "awwww" sounds and breathing slowly. Notice how this feels; you're literally speaking to your nervous system in the language of safety.

Journal Prompts for Deeper Reflection

1. **Safety Discoveries:** What did you discover when you tried the "If I felt safe, I would feel..." exercise? How does it feel to imagine these sensations?
2. **Body Partnership:** If your body could speak, what would it want you to know about how to better care for and listen to it?
3. **Soothing Touch:** How does it feel to offer yourself gentle, nurturing touch combined with soothing sounds? What comes up for you?
4. **Memory Updates:** Can you think of a current situation that activates your nervous system? How might approaching it with your new safety templates change your experience?
5. **Healing Legacy:** What do you hope future generations inherit from your body-based healing work?

11

Modeling Peace

Teaching Through Your Own Healing

The most powerful teaching you will ever do happens not through your words, but through your presence. Every time you choose to breathe instead of react, pause to regulate yourself before responding, or return to your green zone after being activated, you are teaching everyone around you that peace is possible, right now. Not at some future time, but within minutes of being fully charged in your red zone!

This is what I call "modeling peace," and it's perhaps the most important gift you can give to the children and loved ones in your life. You're not just managing your own nervous system - you're demonstrating that emotional regulation is learnable, that overwhelming feelings don't have to lead to overwhelming actions, and that there's always a way back to calm. You can do it!

The Power of the Pause

Let me tell you about one of the most transformative moments in my own parenting journey. I was in the middle of what was escalating into a typical argument with my daughter when I suddenly noticed my arm gesturing in a way that reminded me of my own father when he was angry.

At that moment, instead of continuing down the familiar path of escalation, I stopped mid-sentence and said, "Time out, Honey. Dad needs a time out. I am so sorry, I'm having a right brain flood, honey. I need a few minutes."

I went and lay down for about 10 minutes, did my breathing, and came back to address the situation from my nearly green zone. When I started to speak, I noticed I still wasn't quite right, so I asked for another ten minutes. My family was still in shock so they nodded their heads, silently in agreement.

Later we had a wonderful family meeting. A door opened that had never been opened before. I took ownership of my right brain flood while it was happening. This caused tremendous hope and excitement in my loved ones. It was kind of like doing surgery on myself; challenging, counterintuitive, but so worth it. I stopped the madness.

Even later, I heard my daughter talking to her boyfriend on the phone saying, "I couldn't believe it. There he was, getting ready to blow up and all of a sudden he stopped himself and watched his arm and finger pointing at me, and he said, "Ummm. I am so sorry. I need a 'Time out' and he said he was sorry he was having a right brain flood. Later he came back and asked for more time. Much later we had a very calm family discussion."

She continued, "It was true I did break the window, and I don't even mind paying for it, because my dad was so nice to me. He just stopped yelling. I felt so much love for him. He was really going and he noticed what he was doing and stopped being mean. I want to be just like him."

That pause - that willingness to stop the world and say "I need to regulate myself" - taught my daughter more about emotional intelligence, and what I am striving for, than any lecture ever could have.

What Children Really Learn

Children don't learn emotional regulation from what we tell them about managing feelings. They learn it from watching how we actually handle our own emotions when we're under stress.

If we consistently model that upset feelings lead to upset actions - yelling, blaming, punishing, withdrawing - that's what they learn is normal, appropriate, and becomes their embedded patterns.

But when we model that upset feelings can be acknowledged, that we can take responsibility for our own regulation, and that there's always a way back to connection, that's what they learn is possible for them, too.

Instead of trying to stop the emotional experience or fix it immediately, I was modeling how to be present with difficult emotions without being overwhelmed by them in a hostile way.

The Foster Care Example

This modeling is especially crucial in foster and adoptive families. Children who enter care have often learned from their earliest experiences that adults become dangerous when they're upset, that emotional expression leads to punishment or abandonment, or that there's no such thing as repair after conflict.

When foster parents can model a different way of being with emotions, they're literally rewiring children's understanding of what's possible in relationships.

I worked with a foster father who learned to say, "Wow, my kid's really agitated. I used to think, 'I gotta get him in his green zone.' I was trying to get him there but I now know I cannot do that for him. I have to teach him how he can get in his own green zone, and the only way for me to do that is for me to be in mine."

Instead of seeing the child's activation as a problem to be solved, he saw it as an opportunity to demonstrate regulation and teach co-regulation skills.

What Modeling Peace Looks Like

Modeling peace doesn't mean being perfect or never getting upset. In fact, children need to see that adults have big feelings too, and that those feelings are manageable.

Modeling peace looks like:

Acknowledging when you're activated: "I notice I'm feeling really tense right now."

Taking responsibility for your regulation: "I need to take a few minutes to breathe and calm down."

Not making decisions from activated states: "I'm too upset to have this conversation right now. Let's talk when I'm calmer."

Demonstrating repair: "I'm sorry I raised my voice earlier. I was overwhelmed, and that's not your fault."

Showing that feelings pass: "I was really angry an hour ago, but I feel much calmer now."

The Language of Modeling

The words you use to narrate your emotional regulation process matter. You're teaching children the vocabulary for their own internal experiences.

Instead of: "I'm fine" (when you're clearly not)
Try: "I notice I'm feeling upset, and I'm taking time to sit with it"
Instead of: "You're making me angry"
Try: "I'm noticing I'm getting angry, and I am breathing into it"
Instead of: "Stop crying"
Try: "I can see you have big feelings. I'm going to stay calm while you feel them"

Kerry's Insight About Boundaries

Kerry, one of my students, had a beautiful realization about modeling healthy boundaries. She shared that she and her niece had learned to say "I don't want to talk about it right now, but we'll come back to it later."

This models several crucial concepts:

- It's okay to need space when you're activated
- You can take care of your own needs without abandoning others
- Difficult conversations are worth having when everyone is regulated
- Repair and reconnection are always possible

The Difference Between Suppression and Regulation

It's important to understand that modeling peace is not the same as suppressing your emotions or pretending everything is fine when it isn't. Children can sense when adults are stuffing their feelings, and this can actually increase their anxiety. In fact, we can all sense it in others. This is an example of our vagus nerve sensing the environment.

Emotional suppression teaches, "Feelings are dangerous and must be hidden."
Emotional regulation teaches, "Feelings are normal and manageable."

When you acknowledge your emotions while demonstrating that you can work with them skillfully, you're showing others that they don't need to be afraid of their own emotional experiences.

Greg's Breathing Discovery

My student, Greg, learned that simply saying, "I need to take a step back and take some breaths" was powerful modeling for his family. But as we worked together, he refined this to focus specifically on the exhale, which is where the nervous system regulation actually happens. His children began to notice the difference between the Dad who was tense and reactive, versus the Dad who was breathing and calm. They started asking him to "do the breathing thing" when they could sense his stress escalating.

Other students, Victor and his husband, Trevor, started having breathing circles in the evenings before bedtime. The whole crew lay on the floor on a big blanket with their heads all in the middle near each other in a circle. They would take turns reading the breathing exercises aloud. Their youngest child wanted to participate, but since she couldn't yet read; they recorded her saying, "breathe into fullness and out to complete emptiness" in her cute young voice. Everyone giggled when they listened to her, but it worked for all of them. It will work for your family, too.

Working with Your Own Triggers

Modeling peace requires ongoing awareness of your own triggers and patterns. This isn't about becoming trigger-free (which isn't realistic), but about developing the skill to recognize when you're activated and choose your response consciously.

Some questions that support this awareness:

- What situations consistently negatively and positively activate my nervous system?
- What are my early warning signs that I'm moving out of my green zone?
- What helps me return to regulation most quickly?
- How can I communicate my needs without blaming others?

The Legacy Gift

When you model nervous system regulation for the children in your life, you're giving them what I call "the legacy gift" - the knowledge of how to stay grounded and connected in, spite of what's going on around them.

This is different from developing a thick skin that comes from hardening yourself against life's challenges. This is resilience that comes from knowing how to work with your own nervous system, how to find your way back to peace, your green zone, when you get overwhelmed, and how to maintain connection with others even during difficult times.

Cultural and Generational Patterns

Many of us grew up in families or cultures where emotional expression was discouraged, where "strength" meant not showing feelings, or where conflict was handled through aggression, withdrawal, or passive-aggression.

When you model a different way of being with emotions, you're not just changing your own life - you're interrupting generational patterns and creating new possibilities for how your family handles stress and conflict.

The Practice of Repair

One of the most powerful aspects of modeling peace is demonstrating repair - the ability to come back after conflict and reconnect with love and accountability.

Children need to see that:

- Adults make mistakes and can admit them
- Relationships can be repaired after ruptures
- Love doesn't disappear when people disagree
- It's possible to take responsibility without shame

This might sound like: "I'm sorry I got so frustrated earlier. That wasn't about you - I was overwhelmed with work stuff. How are you feeling about what happened?" Or, "I interpreted you being late as not caring about me, I know that's not true. Are you ok?"

Working with Partner Differences

If you're parenting with a partner, you might find that you have different nervous system patterns and different approaches to regulation. This can actually be a gift if you can work with it consciously.

Maybe one of you tends toward fight responses while the other tends toward flight. Maybe one of you needs alone time to regulate while the other needs connection. When you can model for children how two different nervous systems can work together respectfully, you're teaching them that there are many ways to be human. To do this, you must take turns being the gardener and the flower in the garden, tending to one another, thoughtfully.

When Modeling Feels Hard

Sometimes the pressure to "model peace" can feel overwhelming, especially when you're dealing with your own trauma history or chronic stress. Remember that modeling doesn't require perfection - it requires authenticity and accountability.

Children benefit more from seeing an adult struggle with emotional regulation while trying to do better than from seeing an adult who appears to have no emotions at all.

It's okay to say things like:

- "This is really hard for me because of my own experiences growing up"
- "I'm still learning how to handle big feelings"
- "I made a mistake, and I'm working on doing better next time"

The Long View

Remember that modeling peace is a long-term practice, not a short-term strategy. You won't see immediate changes in children's behavior, and you'll have days when you don't model anything close to peace.

What matters is the overall pattern you're creating - the general message that emotional regulation is possible, that repair is always available, and that love persists through all of life's ups and downs.

Building Your Modeling Practice

Here are some ways to strengthen your ability to model peace:

Develop your own regulation skills first: You can't teach what you don't have. Prioritize your own nervous system health.

Practice during calm moments: Use ordinary interactions to practice regulation skills so they're available during crisis moments.

Get curious about your patterns: Notice what situations tend to activate you and prepare for them when possible.

Create family language: Develop shared vocabulary for talking about nervous system states and regulation needs.

Celebrate progress: Notice and acknowledge when you handle situations differently than you would have in the past.

The children in your life are always watching and learning. When you choose to model peace through your own healing and regulation, you're not just managing the moment - you're creating a legacy of emotional intelligence that will ripple forward through generations.

Your healing is not just personal - it's generational. Every time you break a pattern of reactivity, choose consciousness over unconsciousness, or model that peace is possible, you're changing the world one nervous system at a time.

In our final chapter, we'll explore how to build the support systems that make this profound work sustainable over the long term.

Exercise: Modeling Peace in Action
- Recall a recent moment of stress with someone close to you.
- How did you respond? Did you model peace or reactivity?
- If you could do it again, what would you say or do differently?
- Try narrating your emotional state aloud ("I need a minute to calm down"). Notice the effect.

Journal Prompts for Deeper Reflection
1. **Role Modeling:** Who modeled emotional regulation for you growing up? How did that impact you?

2. **Teaching by Example:** How do you want to model peace for others now?
3. **Repair Rituals:** What is your process for repairing after conflict? How could you make it more intentional?
4. **Family Language:** What phrases or signals would you like to use to talk about emotions and regulation?
5. **Peace Legacy:** What do you hope people remember about your presence during stressful times?

12

Building Your Support Village

You Don't Have to Do This Alone

One of the most damaging myths in our culture is that healing and growth are individual endeavors - that if you're strong enough, skilled enough, or trying hard enough, you should be able to manage everything on your own. This myth is not only false, it's actually harmful to your nervous system, which is designed to co-regulate in relationship with others.

The truth is that healing happens in community. Co-regulation requires other nervous systems to co-regulate with. The strongest, most resilient people I know are not those who need no one; they are those who have built supportive networks of relationships that help them stay grounded and connected, especially during challenging times.

The physiology of connection makes us fundamentally social creatures. Our nervous systems literally develop in relationship with other nervous systems, starting from the moment we're conceived. We learn how to regulate our emotions, how to feel safe in the world, and how to navigate stress through our early relationships with our caregivers.

This means that when we try to heal trauma or manage chronic stress in isolation, we're working against our basic physiology. Your nervous system doesn't just prefer connection - it requires it for optimal functioning.

When you're in your green zone and connecting with others who are also regulated, you reinforce each other's well-being. When you're activated and connecting with someone who's grounded, their nervous system can help yours settle. This is why the right relationships can be literally healing.

Rebecca's Army of One
Rebecca, the student who described herself as "an army of one," was carrying the exhausting burden of trying to manage everything alone. Her depleted happiness hormone scores and chronic overwhelm weren't just personal struggles - they were the predictable result of operating without adequate support.

When Rebecca began to understand that asking for help wasn't weakness but physiological necessity, it opened up new possibilities. "I still have no idea how I'm going to cut down all these incredible obligations," she shared, "but it gives me great hope."

We didn't stop there. I asked her, "in what ways have you taught your family to leave everything up to you?" This question opened her eyes to the myriad ways she took control of everything. She actually inadvertently disempowered everyone around her. They learned to go to her for everything and I mean everything. Once she ended up in the hospital for severe abdominal pain. Her sixteen-year-old called her and asked her how he was supposed to get to basketball practice that day. She was livid. She screamed at him, "I'm in the hospital! Why are you calling me?"

That was the turning point for her. She started examining the ways she was her family's "fixer" and stopped fixing everything. It came from, you guessed it, an early pattern developed in her childhood with parents who rarely attended to her or her needs. She grew up with the vow to attend to her kids when she became a parent. But her vow took her too far and set up the exact same situation for herself as she had when she was a child: family members who did not attend to her or her needs at all.

A few months later she called me and told me something she was very proud of: her son, now seventeen, asked her for permission to take a community college course while in high school. Her initial thought was, "He can't even take out the garbage regularly, how can he manage this?" But she learned how to place a speed bump in between her thoughts and what came out of her mouth. She asked him, "Honey, do you really think you can handle it? You'll have to keep up with your chores and get yourself to the college, I can't help you with any of it."

He was ready for her. He outlined the chart he made for himself, just like the one she has on the fridge with everything she needed to do that week for the other kids in terms of soccer practice, violin lessons, tutoring, etc. Rebecca was truly impressed. She said to him, "Honey, if you think you can do it, I support you 100%."

Later she overheard him talking to a friend on the phone. He was so happy; not because she said "yes" but because she believed in him. Every person has to manage their own nervous system. Every person has to follow through on their own ideas and learn from their mistakes; this is how we grow. It doesn't matter if we succeed or fail at any one thing, because it isn't actually the outcome that matters long term. What matters is how we managed our nervous system and were able to go more deeply into the task or realize it wasn't what we wanted in the first place.

Types of Support Your Nervous System Needs

Not all support is created equal when it comes to nervous system health. Here are different types of support that contribute to your overall well-being:

Emotional Regulation Support: These are people who can help you co-regulate when you're activated. They stay calm when you're upset, offer presence without trying to fix you, and help you find your way back to your green zone.

Practical Support: These are people who can help with concrete tasks and responsibilities, reducing the load on your nervous system by taking care of things that need to be done.

Informational Support: These are people who have knowledge, skills, or experiences that can help you navigate challenges more effectively.

Social Connection: These are relationships that provide joy, laughter, shared interests, and the simple pleasure of human connection.

Professional Support: These are trained helpers like therapists, counselors, medical providers, or other professionals who can offer specialized assistance.

Kerry's Village Approach

Kerry, one of my students, demonstrated beautiful village-building when she talked about doing breathing and yoga practices with her niece. She was creating what I call "regulation partnerships" - relationships where people support each other's nervous system health.

Kerry also mentioned setting up agreements where either person could say, "I don't want to talk about it right now, but we'll come back to it later." This kind of explicit agreement about how to handle activation is an example of creating supportive relationship structures.

Sometimes, when there is a heated discussion or argument, and one person says, "I don't want to talk about it right now," the other person is still charged and has a hard time letting it go. As hard as this is, it is essential to have an agreement of mutual understanding, that when one of you says, "I don't want to talk about it now," that that is the signal which means, "I am having a right brain flood right now and I will probably say things I may not mean because of it. I need some time to cool off." When people are charged, it is difficult to be succinct in this way. Talk with your loved ones and come up with your signal, then do your best to honor it in the moment.

The Caregiver's Dilemma

Caregivers often struggle with building support because they're so focused on giving to others that they forget they need receiving, too. This creates what I call "caregiver depletion" - a state where you're frequently outputting energy and support without enough input to sustain yourself.

Giving is not receiving. You cannot give what you do not possess yourself. This is called "false giving" and many of us got taught to do so at our own personal expense. If you think about it, we receive before we give; it's how we start our lives. What is the very first thing we do when we are born? We cry. But, what has to happen to be able to let out our first cry? We have to breathe in; the deeper the breath, the louder and longer the victory cry. We receive the breath of life before we give our first I AM HERE! You know that silence after a child falls down? The length of the silence is the indicator of how scared or painful the experience was for them. Think about the ways you and your loved ones indicate various kinds of pain.

Practicing being in your green zone is achieved by breathing yourself there consciously. Our breath is our fortitude. Our breath is our recovery. It allows us to communicate with others, and it allows us to hear the voice of God within. You can hear it, too!

Assessing Your Current Village

Take a moment to think about your current support network:

Who helps you feel calm when you're upset? These are your emotional regulation partners.

Who can you call for practical help when you're overwhelmed? These are your practical support people.

Who makes you laugh or brings joy to your life? These are your social connection people.

Who do you trust with your deepest struggles? These are your emotional intimacy people.

What professional support do you have access to? This might include medical providers, therapists, spiritual advisors, or other professionals.

If you're finding gaps in these areas, that's valuable information about where to focus your village-building efforts.

Creating Regulation Partnerships

One of the most powerful types of support you can develop is what I call "regulation partnerships" - relationships where people explicitly support each other's nervous system health.

This might look like:

- Agreeing to breathe together when one person is activated
- Taking turns offering calm presence when the other is upset
- Checking in regularly about stress levels and regulation needs
- Creating signals for when someone needs co-regulation support
- Practicing nervous system skills together during calm times

Rachel and Andrew, the married couple from my class, were developing this kind of partnership by sharing their activity analyses with each other and learning about each other's nervous system patterns. We are both the gardener and a flower in the garden. We have to tend to both ourselves and each other for maximum health and vitality.

The Foster Care Village

Foster and adoptive families especially need robust support villages because they're dealing with complex trauma while trying to provide healing for children. The traditional nuclear family model simply isn't adequate for the level of support needed.

Successful foster families often create extended support networks that might include:

- Other foster families who understand the unique challenges
- Family partners who want to practice the skills in this book together
- Trauma-informed therapists and counselors
- Respite care providers who can offer breaks when needed
- Educational advocates who understand special needs
- Community members who can offer practical support

Working with Professional Support

Professional support isn't just for crisis situations - it can be an ongoing part of your village that helps you maintain wellness and continue growing.

This might include:

- Trauma-informed therapists for processing difficult experiences
- Somatic practitioners for body-based healing work
- Medical providers who understand the physical effects of stress
- Spiritual advisors for meaning-making and connection
- Life coaches for goal-setting and accountability

The key is finding professionals who understand trauma and nervous system functioning, not just those who focus on symptom management.

Building Village When You're Starting from Isolation

If you're currently isolated or don't feel like you have adequate support, building a village can feel overwhelming. Start small:

Identify one person who might be capable of offering some type of support, even if it's limited.

Practice asking for small things before asking for bigger support. This helps you build the skill of receiving help.

Look for community resources like support groups, classes, or volunteer opportunities where you might meet like-minded people.

Consider online communities if in-person connections feel too challenging initially.

Work on your own regulation skills so you can be available for reciprocal relationships when opportunities arise.

The Reciprocity Factor

Healthy support networks involve reciprocity - everyone both gives and receives. If you're someone who's comfortable giving but struggles with receiving, building a village will require learning to accept help gracefully. If you're someone who tends to take more than you give, building a village will require developing your capacity to offer support to others. The goal is creating relationships where support flows both ways, where everyone feels valued and cared for, and where the giving and receiving happen naturally over time rather than being perfectly balanced in every interaction.

Boundaries in Your Village

Having a support village doesn't mean everyone has unlimited access to you or that you're responsible for managing everyone else's nervous system. Healthy villages require clear boundaries.

This might include:

- Being clear about what kinds of support you can and cannot offer
- Communicating your own needs and limitations honestly
- Recognizing when someone's support needs exceed what you can provide

- Knowing when to refer people to professional help; you can tell when this is by paying attention to the quality of your internal physical sensations.
- Protecting your own regulation so you can be available to others

Remember, you can't pour from an empty cup. Taking care of your own nervous system isn't selfish - it's what allows you to be genuinely helpful to others.

Virtual Villages

In our increasingly connected world, your support village doesn't have to be geographically limited. Online communities, video calls with distant friends, and digital support groups can all be valuable parts of your nervous system support network.

The key is finding ways to create genuine connection and co-regulation, even through screens. This might mean:

- Video calls where you can see each other's faces and body language
- Voice-only calls where you can hear breathing and tone
- Synchronized activities like breathing or meditation together online
- Regular check-ins that focus on nervous system states, not just life updates

Village During Crisis

The real test of your support village comes during crisis moments - times of illness, job loss, family emergencies, or other significant stressors. These are the times when your nervous system most needs co-regulation support.

Having conversations about crisis support before you need it can be incredibly helpful:

- Who can you call at 2:00 am if you're having a panic attack?
- Who can help with practical needs if you're overwhelmed?
- What kind of support do you find most helpful during difficult times?
- How can others best support you without overwhelming you further?

Teaching Children About the Village

One of the most important gifts you can give children is helping them understand that they don't have to manage life alone. Children who grow up understanding that support is available and normal are more likely to seek help when they need it as adults.

This might look like:

- Modeling asking for help when you need it
- Talking about the different people in your support network
- Helping children identify their own support people
- Teaching children how to offer age-appropriate support to others
- Celebrating the ways your family supports each other

Common Village-Building Challenges

"I don't want to be a burden": Remember that offering support to others is often meaningful and fulfilling for them. You're not just taking when you accept help - you're giving others the opportunity to contribute.

"I should be able to handle this myself": This cultural myth keeps people isolated and struggling unnecessarily. Needing support is human, not weak.

"I don't have time for relationships": Relationships aren't another item on your to-do list - they're what makes everything else sustainable.

"People always let me down": Past disappointments can make it hard to trust new relationships. Start small and build slowly.

"I don't know how to ask for help": This is a learnable skill. Start with small requests and practice being specific about what you need.

Maintaining Your Village

Support villages require ongoing attention and care. Like gardens, they need regular tending to stay healthy and flourishing.

This might include:

- Regular check-ins with key support people
- Expressing gratitude for support received
- Offering support proactively, not just when asked
- Addressing conflicts or misunderstandings quickly
- Adjusting the level of connection based on changing life circumstances
- Adding new people to your village as you grow and change

The Professional Village Addition

Sometimes your village needs to include professional support to address specific challenges or provide specialized help. This isn't a sign of failure - it's a sign of wisdom.

Professional support might be especially important if:

- You're dealing with complex trauma that requires specialized treatment
- You have mental health conditions that benefit from medication or therapy
- You're facing challenges that require specific expertise
- Your support needs exceed what friends and family can reasonably provide

Creating Village for Your Whole Family

When you have children, part of building your village involves creating support for them, too. This might include:

- Teachers who understand your child's needs
- Friends' families where your children feel welcome
- Extended family members who can offer different types of connection
- Professional support for children when needed
- Community activities that build social connections

The Long View of Village Building

Building a support village is not a quick fix or a one-time project. It's an ongoing practice that evolves throughout your life as your needs change and as you grow in your capacity to both give and receive support.

Some relationships will be lifelong, others will be seasonal. Some people will provide deep emotional support, others will be wonderful companions for specific activities. Some will be available for crisis support, others will be your everyday social connection.

The diversity of your village is part of its strength. You don't need one person who meets all your needs - you need a network of people who collectively help you thrive.

Your Village as a Gift to Others

When you build a strong support village for yourself, you're not just serving your own needs - you're becoming a more available and regulated person who can offer better support to others.

When your own nervous system is well-supported, you can be present for your children's needs without depleting yourself. When you have adequate practical support, you can offer emotional support to friends. When you feel connected and valued, you can extend that connection to others who are isolated.

Your village becomes a model for others of what's possible. When people see you receiving and giving support naturally, they learn that this kind of community is available to them too.

Starting Today
Building a support village starts with small steps. Today, you might:

- Reach out to one person you haven't connected with in a while
- Ask for help with one small thing you've been struggling with alone
- Offer specific support to someone in your life
- Join one group or activity where you might meet like-minded people
- Express gratitude to someone who has supported you

Remember, you're not trying to build a perfect village overnight. You're taking one step toward connection, toward community, toward the biological reality that healing happens in relationship.

The village you build will be unique to you, reflecting your personality, your needs, your interests, and your capacity. Trust yourself to know what kinds of support feel nourishing versus draining, what level of connection feels right versus overwhelming.

Your nervous system knows what it needs to feel safe and supported. Your job is to listen to that wisdom and take action to create the connections that will help you not just survive, but truly thrive.

Exercise: Village Mapping
- Draw a map of your current support network ("village").
- Who can you call for practical help, emotional support, fun, or advice?
- Where are the gaps?
- Identify one area where you'd like more support and brainstorm small steps to build it.

Journal Prompts for Deeper Reflection
1. **Support Inventory:** Who are your "anchors" and "builders" in your life right now?
2. **Receiving Help:** How do you feel about asking for or accepting help? What beliefs shape this?
3. **Reciprocity:** How do you balance giving and receiving support?
4. **Village Growing:** What small step could you take this week to strengthen your support network?
5. **Modeling Community:** How can you show others (especially children) that it's healthy to ask for and offer support?

Conclusion: Your Legacy of Healing

The Ripples That Extend Beyond You

As we come to the end of our journey together through this book, I want you to pause for a moment and consider something profound: every time you have chosen to breathe instead of react, every moment you have paused to notice your nervous system and respond with compassion, every instance where you have moved from your red zone back to your green zone, you have been doing more than taking care of yourself.

You have been changing the world.

This might sound dramatic, but I mean it literally. When you learn to regulate your own nervous system, you become someone who can stay grounded during life's storms. When you model that peace is possible even in difficult moments, you create ripples that extend far beyond your own life.

The Story of Change

Let me tell you about Maria, a former foster youth I worked with several years ago. She came to my classes angry, defensive, and convinced that the world was fundamentally unsafe. Her nervous system had learned through painful experience that adults were unpredictable, that expressing needs led to catastrophic disappointment, and that the safest strategy was to trust no one.

Maria was skeptical of everything I taught. She rolled her eyes at the breathing exercises, scoffed at the idea that she could influence her own brain chemistry, and insisted that positive thinking was "fake toxic positivity for people who've never experienced real problems."

But something shifted when I introduced the polyvagal chart and helped her understand that her rage and defensiveness weren't character flaws - they were her nervous system's brilliant protective strategies. For the first time, someone was telling her that her responses made perfect sense.

Slowly, Maria began experimenting with the 4-10 breathing technique. Not because she believed it would work, but because she was curious about this scientific switch I kept talking about. She started noticing her yellow zone signals and practicing moving back to green before she hit the red zone.

The transformation was gradual but profound. Maria began to see that she had choices about how to respond to stress. She learned that her nervous system could be her ally rather than her enemy. Most importantly, she discovered that she could feel her feelings without being overwhelmed by them.

But here's the best part of Maria's story: the changes didn't stop with her. When Maria moved in with her grandmother, she taught her grandmother the breathing techniques. When her younger brother came to visit, she helped him understand why he felt so scared all the time and showed him how to calm his nervous system.

Maria became a peer counselor for other foster youth, teaching them the same nervous system skills that had transformed her own life. She started a support group where young people could practice co-regulation together. She became living proof that healing is possible, that trauma doesn't have to define your future, and that you can break generational patterns.

Today, Maria is a social worker specializing in trauma-informed care. She's married to someone who understands nervous system regulation, and they're raising their children with these tools from the very beginning. The ripples of her healing continue to spread.

Your Own Ripple Effect

You might be thinking, "But I'm not a social worker or peer counselor. I'm just someone trying to get through my daily life without losing my mind."

Here's what I want you to understand: you don't have to have a professional helping role to create powerful ripples of healing. Every relationship you're in, every interaction you have, every moment when you choose regulation over reactivity, you are teaching others what's possible.

When you breathe yourself back to calm instead of escalating during an argument with your partner, you're showing them that de-escalation is possible.

When you pause to regulate yourself instead of yelling at your children when they're being difficult, you're teaching them that big feelings don't have to lead to big actions.

When you stay grounded while a friend is having a crisis, you're offering them the co-regulation that helps their nervous system remember how to settle.

When you practice self-compassion instead of self-criticism when you make mistakes, you're modeling for everyone around you that healing is possible.

Even though you now completely understand these concepts, it's still likely that you are going to end up in your red zone. It's likely you will get into fights or have miscommunications. You're family will still get on your nerves. You will get on their nerves as well. The main thing is that as soon as you notice, that's when you apply the concepts in this book. Keep offering your nervous system new ideas, imagine better outcomes, and keep coming back to your own green zone. The deeper your training, the longer it takes to rework your neural pathways; but it's worth it.

The Children Are Watching

The children in your life - whether they're your own children, foster children, nieces and nephews, students, or neighborhood kids - are constantly learning from your example. They're not just listening to what you say about emotions and stress management; they're absorbing how you actually handle your own emotions and stress.

When children see an adult notice they're getting activated, take a pause, breathe themselves back to regulation, and then return to the situation from a calm place, they learn something revolutionary: that emotional overwhelm is temporary, that there are tools to work with difficult feelings, and that relationships can be repaired after conflict.

These children grow up with a completely different understanding of what's possible than children who only see adults react from their red zones. They learn that feelings are manageable, that stress is workable, and that peace is always available.

They become adults who know how to regulate their own nervous systems, who can co-regulate with others during difficult times, and who can teach these same skills to their own children. This is how generational healing happens.

Breaking the Cycles

For many of us, learning nervous system regulation means breaking cycles that have been present in our families for generations. Cycles of trauma, cycles of reactivity, cycles of emotional unavailability, cycles of conflict without repair.

Every time you choose a different response than the one that was modeled for you, you're interrupting those cycles. Every time you stay regulated when your family of origin would have gotten activated, you're creating new patterns. Every time you repair a relationship rupture instead of letting it fester, you're demonstrating new possibilities.

This work isn't just about you feeling better (though that matters tremendously). This work is about changing the trajectory of your family line, about ensuring that future generations have different tools and different possibilities available to them.

The Professional Ripples

If you work in any helping profession - education, healthcare, social services, law enforcement, religious leadership - learning nervous system regulation transforms not just your personal life but your professional effectiveness.

Teachers who understand nervous system regulation can recognize when students are in their red zones and need co-regulation support rather than disciplinary consequences.

Healthcare providers who can stay regulated themselves provide better care and can help anxious patients settle their nervous systems.

Social workers who understand trauma and nervous system functioning can offer families the tools they need to heal rather than just managing crises.

The ripples extend throughout entire systems when people in helping roles understand how nervous systems work and can model regulation for the people they serve.

The Community Impact

When you become someone who can stay regulated during community conflicts, neighborhood tensions, or social upheavals, you become part of the "regulating presence" in your broader community.

You become one of the people others turn to when they need help staying regulated. You become someone who can hold space for others' big feelings without getting overwhelmed yourself. You become a source of wisdom about how to work with stress and conflict constructively.

Communities need people who can stay grounded during chaotic times, who can see through the reactivity to the underlying needs and fears, and who can help groups of people find their way back to connection and collaboration.

The Global Perspective

I know it might seem grandiose to suggest that your individual nervous system regulation work contributes to global healing, but I believe it does. The same patterns that create conflict in families create conflict in communities, organizations, and nations.

When people are operating from their red zones - feeling threatened, defensive, and reactive - they make decisions that create more conflict and suffering. When people can stay in their green zones - feeling safe, connected, and collaborative - they make decisions that create more peace and healing.

Every person who learns to regulate their nervous system becomes one more person who can respond to conflict with wisdom rather than reactivity, who can stay connected to their humanity even during difficult times, and who can model that another way is possible.

What You've Learned

Take a moment to reflect on what you've learned through our time together:

You've learned that your difficult emotions aren't character flaws but neurobiological experiences that make perfect sense given your history and current circumstances.

You've learned that you have a sophisticated internal guidance system - your nervous system - that's constantly giving you information about safety and danger, and that learning to listen to this guidance can transform how you navigate life.

You've learned that your breath is medicine, that you can literally change your brain chemistry through how you breathe, and that this tool is always available to you.

You've learned that healing happens in relationships, that you don't have to figure everything out alone, and that building a support village is essential for long-term well-being.

You've learned that your healing is not just personal but generational, that every choice you make toward regulation and peace contributes to breaking cycles and creating new possibilities for the people you love.

Most importantly, you've learned that you can hear the voice of God speaking to you when you are happily located in your own personal green zone.

The Ongoing Journey

This book is ending, but your journey with nervous system regulation is just beginning. This isn't a one-time learning but a lifelong practice. You'll have days when you remember to breathe early in your stress response and easily return to calm. You'll have other days when you're deep in activation before you remember you have these tools.

Both experiences are normal and valuable. The goal isn't perfection - it's developing an increasingly friendly relationship with your own nervous system and increasingly skillful responses to life's inevitable challenges.

Some practices that can support your ongoing journey:

Regular nervous system check-ins: Develop a practice of asking yourself "What zone am I in right now?" several times throughout the day.

Breathing practice: Use the 4-10 breathing technique not just during crisis moments but as preventive medicine during calm times.

Activity analysis: Periodically reassess how your daily activities affect your nervous system and make adjustments as needed.

Support village maintenance: Continue nurturing the relationships that support your regulation and be open to adding new support people as your life evolves.

Learning and growth: Stay curious about nervous system functioning and trauma healing. Read additional books, take classes, work with professionals as needed.

A Personal Promise

Here is my personal promise: if you continue practicing the tools in this book, treating your nervous system with the respect and attention it deserves, if you keep choosing regulation over reactivity even when it's difficult, your life will improve in ways you cannot yet imagine.

Not because these tools are magic, but because they work with your own science. When you support your nervous system's natural capacity for healing and regulation, creating the conditions for your happiness hormones to flow, when you build genuine support connections with others, you unleash your nervous system's innate wisdom and resilience.

You'll find yourself less reactive to things that used to send you spinning. You'll discover reserves of patience and compassion you didn't know you had. You'll become someone others can count on for stability and support. You'll sleep better, connect more deeply, and experience more moments of genuine peace and joy.

Your Legacy Starts Now

Your legacy of healing doesn't start when you've mastered all these skills or when you feel perfectly regulated all the time. Your legacy starts right now, with the next breath you take, the next choice you make to respond rather than react, the next moment you treat yourself with the same compassion you would offer a beloved friend.

Every time you pause to breathe when you notice stress building, you're adding to your legacy.

Every time you stay regulated when someone else is activated, you're adding to your legacy.

Every time you repair a relationship after conflict instead of letting resentment build, you're adding to your legacy.

Every time you model that peace is possible even in difficult moments, you're adding to your legacy.

The Continuing Circle

As you continue this journey, remember that you're part of a larger circle of healing. There are people all over the world who are doing this same work - learning to regulate their nervous systems, healing their trauma, building supportive communities, and modeling peace for the next generation.

You're not alone in this work. Every breath you take toward healing joins with countless other breaths being taken by people who, like you, have decided that breaking cycles of trauma and reactivity is worth the effort.

Your healing contributes to their healing. Their healing contributes to yours. Together, we're creating a world where more children grow up feeling safe, where more adults know how to work with their emotions skillfully, and where more communities can navigate conflict with wisdom rather than reactivity.

A Final Breath Together

As we close our time together, I invite you to take one final conscious breath with me. Breathe in through your nose for a count of four... hold gently... and exhale slowly through your mouth for a count of ten, letting everything go. Or breathe into fullness and out to complete emptiness.

In this moment, notice that you are okay. Notice that you have survived everything that has happened to you so far. Notice that you have within you everything you need to heal, to grow, and to create the life you want.

Your breath is your constant companion. Your nervous system is your ally. Your capacity for healing is limitless. God is with you every minute of every day. Your legacy of peace starts now.

Thank you for taking this journey with me. Thank you for having the courage to do this healing work. Thank you for becoming someone who helps make the world a safer, more regulated, more peaceful place.

The ripples of your healing extend far beyond what you can see. Trust that every small step you take toward nervous system health matters, that every moment of regulation you achieve contributes to the healing of the world.

Your healing is a gift - to yourself, to your loved ones, to your community, and to future generations who will benefit from the cycles you choose to break and the new patterns you choose to create.

Breathe on, dear one. Heal on. The world needs exactly what you have to offer when you're grounded in your own green zone, connected to your own wisdom, and committed to your own ongoing healing.

Your journey continues with the next breath you take. I have great faith in you!

Appendix A: Quick Reference Guides

The 4-10 Breathing Technique

1. Exhale with a whoosh and empty your lungs
2. Breathe in through your nose for a count of 4
3. Breathe out through your mouth (like blowing through a straw) for a count of 10
4. During the exhale, completely relax all muscles ("deflate")
5. Repeat until you feel settled in your green zone

Your Nervous System Zones

Green Zone (Safety):

- Calm, settled, grounded
- Curious, open, compassionate
- Present and connected
- Happiness hormones flowing

Yellow Zone (Caution/Fight or Flight):

- Frustration, worry, concern
- Irritation, anxiety
- Anger, fear
- Rage, panic

Red Zone (Life Threat/Freeze):

- Trapped

- Depressed
- Shut Down
- Numb/Disassociation

Happiness Hormones Quick Guide

Dopamine (Achievement): Goal-setting, meaningful action, music, light exercise; "Who did it, I did it!"

Endorphins (Natural high): Intense exercise, laughter, dark chocolate, group activities; "Yes, I can!"

Oxytocin (Connection): Safe touch, quality time, caring for others, gratitude; "Aaaawwww! Patting Chest."

Serotonin (Feel-good): Sunlight, nature, positive thinking, protein-rich foods; "Oooh! I love doing that!"

Co-Regulation Phrases
- "I can see this is really hard for you"
- "Your feelings make sense"
- "I'm going to breathe while you have your feelings"
- "I can see that you're really upset right now"
- "I hear you're not feeling safe right now"
- "This feeling will pass"

For more information about classes, workshops, and the Happiness Hormone Quiz, visit us at:
https://tools4life.net/classes

To Download Activity Analysis Worksheets:
https://tools4life.net/home-worksheets

Appendix B: Resources for Continued Learning

Recommended Reading

- "The Polyvagal Theory" by Stephen Porges, PhD
- "The Body Keeps the Score" by Dr. Bessel van der Kolk
- "Polyvagal Theory in Therapy" by Deb Dana, LCSW
- "The Edinburgh and Dore lectures" by Thomas Troward
- "The Whole-Brain Child" by Dr. Daniel Siegel and Tina Payne Bryson, PhD
- "Living Buddha, Living Christ" and "How to Love" by Thich Nhat Hahn
- "Life Visioning" by Michael Bernard Beckwith
- "This Called Called You" by Ernest Homes
- "What Happened to You?" by Dr. Bruce Perry and Oprah Winfrey

Professional Support Resources

- Emotional Freedom Practitioners: https://tappingthematrixacademy.com/academy-clinic
- Somatic Experiencing practitioners: https://traumahealing.org
- EMDR (Eye Movement Desensitization and Reprocessing) therapy providers: https://emdria.org
- Foster care support: National Foster Parent Association: https://nfpaonline.org

Online Communities and Support Suggestions

- Trauma survivors support groups
- Foster and adoptive parent networks
- Mindfulness and nervous system regulation communities
- Local community mental health resources

Remember: This book provides educational information and practical tools, but it is not a substitute for professional mental health treatment when needed. Please seek appropriate professional support for serious mental health concerns.

Chapter Summaries

Introduction: Your Journey to Wholeness

We begin by acknowledging that if you're reading this, you've likely experienced more than your share of life's challenges. This isn't a book about fixing what's broken - it's about understanding that your responses make perfect sense and learning gentle ways to care for yourself and your loved ones. You'll discover that healing trauma isn't about erasing the past; it's about changing how your nervous system responds to the present.

Chapter 1: The Language of Your Body

Your body is constantly communicating with you through physical sensations. We'll explore how to recognize the difference between feeling safe (calm, relaxed, grounded) and feeling unsafe (tight, heavy, constricted). This isn't about judgment - it's about developing awareness. When you can notice "Oh, I'm feeling that tightness in my jaw again," you can respond with compassion rather than react from fear.

Chapter 2: Your Internal Chemistry

Imagine your body as having two different medicine cabinets - one filled with happiness hormones (dopamine, endorphins, oxytocin, serotonin) and another with stress hormones (cortisol). Your nervous system chooses which medicine to dispense based on whether it perceives safety or danger. This chapter helps you understand that difficult emotions aren't personality flaws - they're your physiology trying to protect you.

Chapter 3: The Dance of Your Brain

Your right brain holds emotions and memories, while your left brain manages logic and language. When you're upset, these two sides stop communicating effectively. This explains why someone might say "just use your words" when you're crying, but you literally can't access words in that moment. Understanding this removes shame and creates space for healing.

Chapter 4: The Power of Interpretation

The most important word in trauma healing is "interpret." Your nervous system responds not to what's actually happening, but to how it interprets what's happening. If your early experiences taught you that raised voices mean danger, your body will react to any raised voice - even joyful excitement - as a threat. This isn't wrong; it's protective. But once you understand this, you can gently retrain your responses.

Chapter 5: Your Nervous System Map

Think of your nervous system like a traffic light. Green means safety - you feel grounded, creative, and connected. Yellow means caution - you might feel frustrated or worried. Red means danger - you're in fight, flight, or freeze mode. The goal isn't to never leave green; it's to notice when you've moved and consciously return to safety.

Chapter 6: The Breath as Medicine

You breathe every moment of every day, so you already have the most powerful healing tool available. The secret is in the exhale - breathing out slowly tells your nervous system that you're safe. We'll explore the 4-10 breathing technique (inhale for 4, exhale for 10) as a way to literally switch off stress hormone production and turn on happiness hormone creation.

Chapter 7: Becoming Your Own Detective

This chapter introduces a gentle way to examine your daily activities and notice which ones create stress versus joy in your body. It's not about judgment, but about awareness. Maybe you'll discover that certain activities drain you unnecessarily, or that small changes could make big differences in how you feel throughout the day.

Chapter 8: Creating Your Happiness Hormone Calendar

Learn to intentionally incorporate activities that support each type of happiness hormone into your week. Monday might be for dopamine (setting and achieving small goals), Tuesday for endorphins (movement and laughter), and so on. This isn't about adding more to your plate - it's about being intentional with what's already there.

Chapter 9: The Art of Co-Regulation

One of the most beautiful aspects of being human is that we naturally sync up with each other's nervous systems. If you're calm, others tend to become calm around you. If you're activated, others often become activated too. This chapter explores how to become the person who helps everyone else feel safer, starting with feeling safe yourself.

Chapter 10: When the Past Lives in Your Body

Trauma isn't what happened to you - it's what happens inside you as a result of what happened to you. Your nervous system learned to protect you in whatever way it could. These protective patterns made perfect sense then, and honoring them while gently creating new patterns makes sense now.

Chapter 11: Modeling Peace

The most powerful gift you can give to those you love is your own healing. When children see an adult notice they're getting upset, take a pause, breathe, and return to calm, they learn that this is possible. They learn that big feelings don't have to lead to big actions. They learn that they, too, can find their way back to peace.

Chapter 12: Building Your Support Village

Healing happens in relationship. This chapter explores how to identify and nurture the relationships that support your nervous system health. Sometimes this means setting boundaries with people who consistently activate your stress response. Sometimes it means reaching out for help. It always means remembering that you don't have to do this alone.

Conclusion: Your Legacy of Healing

Every time you pause to breathe when you notice stress, every time you choose to return to your green zone before responding, every time you treat your own nervous system with gentleness - you're not just healing yourself. You're changing the patterns that get passed down through generations. You're creating a legacy of peace that will ripple forward in ways you may never fully know.

Acknowledgements

I acknowledge the following people and organizations for their contributions to my healing journey; they are my Circle of Beloveds.

Joan Menke, my life coach: Thank you for teaching me how to breathe and restore my own natural balance; for encouraging me to say, "Yes" to opportunities, and to accept failure as feedback and not moral incapacity.

Thomas Hedlund, my therapist: Thank you for giving me the space to unpack my childhood traumas; you helped the sun reach me and grow me into the sunflower I am meant to be.

Thomas Troward, author of *The Edinburgh and Dore Lectures*: Thank you for enlightening me to how God indwells in us through the nervous system. Your work was the catalyst for a whole new level of understanding in me, about me, and in my work with others.

Corina Scherer, Minister, Center for Spiritual Living, Puerto Vallarta, Mexico: Thank you for your gentle way of teaching and supporting me in my personal growth and spiritual education.

Sarah Johnson, my Emotional Freedom Practitioner: Thank you for teaching me how to place a speed bump between my feelings and what comes out of my mouth and to honor my feelings; to say, "I'm not okay right now" and to relish the truth of being honest.

The Redwood Men's Center: Thank you for holding a space for men to "bring our whole selves" to retreats. Your men's work is profound and a blessing.

The Billys: Thank you for being a loving, heart-centered group of men that not only embraces diversity, but celebrates it.

To God: Thank you for everything that has happened in my life. I feel your presence in my every breath. I am well aware that this book is You working through me, and for this I am grateful.

In Gratitude

A special thank you to the following giants whose work has lifted me up personally and professionally:

Dr. Steven Porges
Deb Dana, LCSW
Dr. Daniel Siegel
Tina Payne Bryson, PhD.
Dr. Bessel Van Der Kolk
Ernest Holmes
Thomas Troward

Notes

ABOUT THE AUTHOR

Nick Lawrence, MA, is an educator, trauma specialist, and lifelong student of the human experience. With over thirty years of study in neuroscience, human development, psychology, biology, and metaphysics, Nick is renowned for his ability to break down complex concepts into clear, practical steps. Drawing from his professional expertise and personal journey of healing, Nick has helped countless individuals, families, and caregivers transform their legacy of trauma into a foundation for thriving. His work is grounded in compassion, science, and a deep belief in everyone's capacity to heal. Nick lives his mission every day: helping people come home to themselves and create generational change through nervous system awareness and heart-centered living.

www.ingramcontent.com/pod-product-compliance
Lightning Source LLC
Chambersburg PA
CBHW050341010526
44119CB00049B/643